ESSEX RAILWAYS

WILLIAM H. SMITH

SUTTON PUBLISHING LIMITED

Sutton Publishing Limited
Phoenix Mill · Thrupp · Stroud
Gloucestershire · GL5 2BU

First published 2000

Title page: Clacton-on-Sea 'old' station, *c*. 1905, with a GER bus on the Clacton to St Osyth route in view. The wooden station survived in this form until 1929 when it was rebuilt by the LNER. *(N. Bowdidge Collection)*

British Library Cataloguing in Publication Data
A catalogue record for this book is available from the British Library.

ISBN 0-7509-2309-1

Typeset in 10.5/13.5 Photina.
Typesetting and origination by
Sutton Publishing Limited.
Printed in Great Britain by
Cromwell Press Ltd, Trowbridge, Wiltshire.

Acknowledgements

I would like to thank: Nigel Bowdidge; Roger Carpenter; Richard Casserley; Adrian Corder-Birch and the Essex Family History group; Essex County Record Office staff at Chelmsford, Colchester and Southend; Great Eastern Railway Society; Paul Goldsmith; Historical Model Railway Society; Lens of Sutton; Peter Paton; Dick Riley and Graham Stacey (RAS Marketing)

A number of members of the Great Eastern Railway Society have assisted me greatly with contributions to the photographic content, adding to information contained in the captions, and have compiled and made available an archive of records that may be accessed by members of the Society. However, any errors and omissions are entirely my own.

The Great Eastern Railway Society

The Great Eastern Railway Society was founded in 1973 to promote a widespread interest in the GER, to encourage and co-ordinate research into its history, and to provide a permanent record of the results. Although we are primarily studying the period of the lifespan of the Great Eastern Railway from 1862 to 1922, we also encompass its constituent companies and its successors up to the present day, plus other independent and joint railways in the Eastern counties.

The Society publishes the *Great Eastern Journal* and the *Great Eastern News* quarterly and these are supplied to members only. The *Journal* contains articles, photographs, plans and drawings dealing with the history of the GER and associated railways, and each issue currently contains forty-eight pages or more. The Society keeps in print every one of the 100-plus issues produced so far, so that new members can purchase individual issues of interest, or complete sets. The *Great Eastern News* is a newsletter keeping members informed of matters to do with the Society. Of a similar standard to the *Journal*, it frequently contains photographs and drawings. The number of pages varies from issue to issue, depending upon the current news, but regular items include notices and reports of meetings, book and model reviews, developments on the GER scene today, members' requests for information and assistance and so on.

Apart from the Journal and News, sent free to members, the Society publishes some 400 other items whish are offered for sale. Paramount among these are the GERS Information Sheets which cover subjects such as summaries of Railway Company Board and Committee minute books, copies of staff instructions, rule books, timetables, maps, indexes to reference sources and so on. Other publications include several booklets, scale drawings of locomotives and rolling stock, buildings, etc.

Two general meetings are held in March and October which include talks, slide shows, displays, etc. The Society aims to provide a friendly atmosphere in which people of all ages and from all walks of life can converse and correspond with one another. There are also several local groups which meet regularly, within and outside the GER area, and the Society is keen to promote the formation of further groups.

Membership of the Society is currently around 900, worldwide, and includes practically all of the known authorities of the Railway, and many professional railwaymen. Membership is open to all, and offers scope for a wide range of interests; archivists, historians, modellers and general railway enthusiasts. The subscription to the Great Eastern Railway Society is currently £20 per year. The subscriptions are due on 1 April each year. New members joining the Society receive a Members' Handbook and membership list, plus copies of all issues of the Great Eastern Journal and Great Eastern News published since the beginning of the subscription year. Thus, even if you join the GERS in January, for example, you will receive copies of all publications produced since the previous April.

For more information on the Great Eastern Railway Society and an application form to join, please write to: GERS Membership Secretary, 9 Clare Road, Leytonstone, London, E11 1JU.

CONTENTS

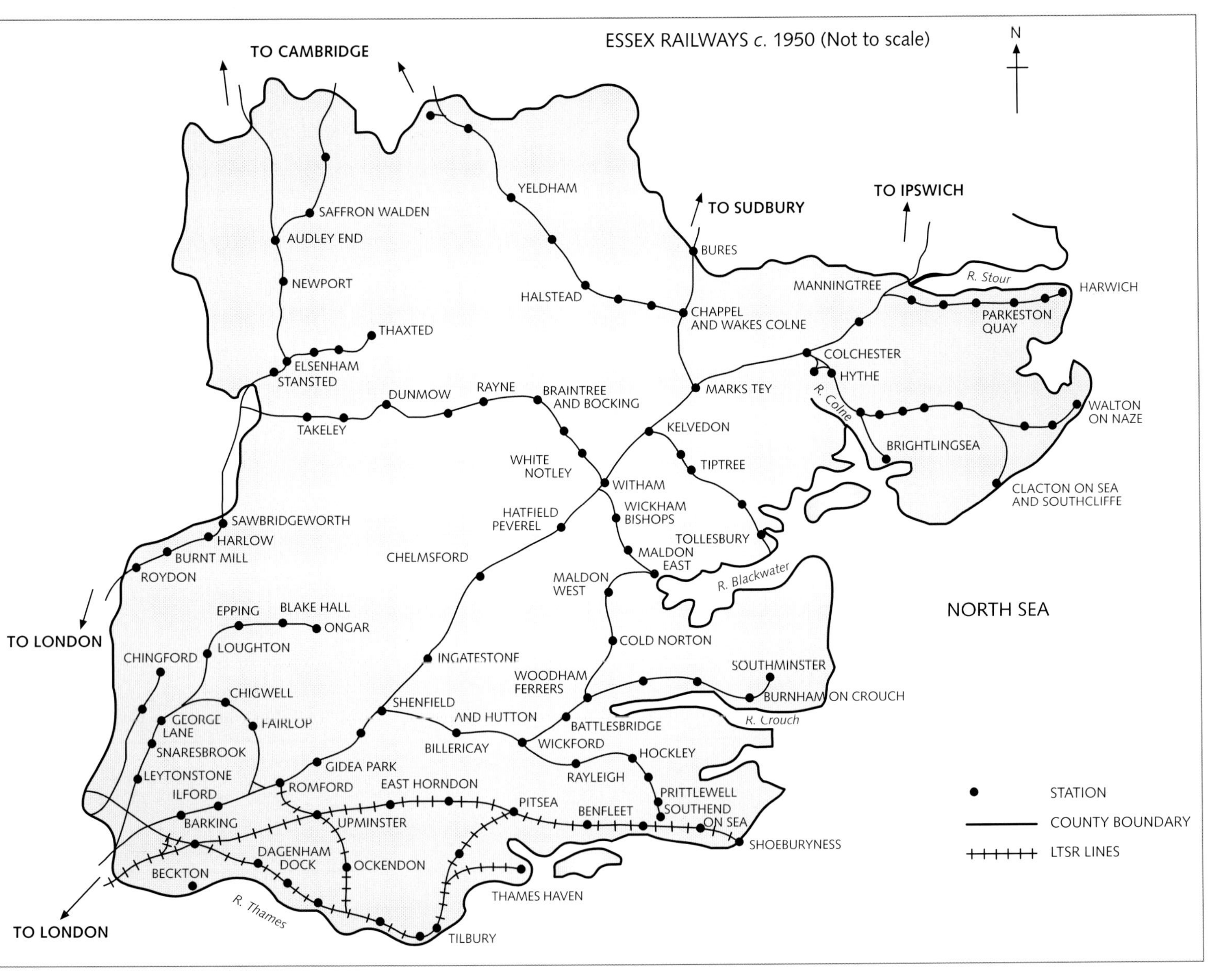
ESSEX RAILWAYS c. 1950 (Not to scale)
N
TO CAMBRIDGE
TO SUDBURY
TO IPSWICH
TO LONDON
TO LONDON
YELDHAM
SAFFRON WALDEN
AUDLEY END
NEWPORT
THAXTED
ELSENHAM
STANSTED
TAKELEY
DUNMOW
RAYNE
BRAINTREE AND BOCKING
WHITE NOTLEY
HALSTEAD
BURES
CHAPPEL AND WAKES COLNE
MANNINGTREE
R. Stour
HARWICH
PARKESTON QUAY
COLCHESTER
HYTHE
R. Colne
MARKS TEY
KELVEDON
TIPTREE
WALTON ON NAZE
BRIGHTLINGSEA
CLACTON ON SEA AND SOUTHCLIFFE
WITHAM
WICKHAM BISHOPS
TOLLESBURY
MALDON EAST
R. Blackwater
MALDON WEST
HATFIELD PEVEREL
CHELMSFORD
SAWBRIDGEWORTH
HARLOW
BURNT MILL
ROYDON
EPPING
BLAKE HALL
ONGAR
LOUGHTON
CHINGFORD
CHIGWELL
GEORGE LANE
FAIRLOP
SNARESBROOK
LEYTONSTONE
ILFORD
BARKING
ROMFORD
GIDEA PARK
SHENFIELD
AND HUTTON
BILLERICAY
INGATESTONE
COLD NORTON
WOODHAM FERRERS
SOUTHMINSTER
BURNHAM ON CROUCH
R. Crouch
BATTLESBRIDGE
WICKFORD
HOCKLEY
RAYLEIGH
PRITTLEWELL
SOUTHEND ON SEA
SHOEBURYNESS
BENFLEET
PITSEA
EAST HORNDON
UPMINSTER
DAGENHAM DOCK
OCKENDON
BECKTON
R. Thames
THAMES HAVEN
TILBURY
NORTH SEA
STATION
COUNTY BOUNDARY
LTSR LINES

INTRODUCTION

In the 1830s surveyors and engineers were moving across Essex preparing plans for the birth of a railway system that was to make significant differences to the way people lived. As schemes were financially underwritten and then granted powers in Parliament, the railway contractors followed the planners so that, by the 1840s, the sights and sounds of the Essex countryside would include, in some places, the exertions of the itinerant gangs of navvies who were busy shaping the trackbed ready for the permanent way. These railway developments set in motion dramatic alterations to the speed at which people and their products could be moved, thereby providing the catalyst for major social and economic changes.

Previously the stagecoach, cart, packhorse and the droving of livestock were the only facilities of transport by land for long journeys, while coastal shipping, river and canal navigation could only deal slowly with the movement of bulky goods. As well as speed, railway transport offered access, convenience and opportunities in both employment and investment. For the majority of the population the railways brought an improved standard of living and broke down much of the isolation to be found in rural Essex.

Towards the end of the era popularly called the 'railway mania', the 1840s and '50s, Essex was left with connecting railway services based upon main trunk routes between the larger towns. By the 1870s the railways of Essex were spreading in all directions as branchlines reached small villages, and inter-connecting minor routes were established across an agricultural landscape already showing many changes as a result of the new possibilities that railway transport had encouraged.

At a time when 'coal was king', and with no mineral deposits in the county, one company, the Great Eastern Railway, had evolved to become the major provider of fuel sources in Essex. It also became the major force in an increased mobility of labour which continued to cause great social and economic upheaval as it became possible to look for employment outside the home village. The GER was the outcome of a financial rescue plan in 1862, thereby amalgamating five pioneering companies which had each overstretched their own resources.

After an uncertain beginning, by 1874 the GER directors had retrieved a possible company disaster and had ambitions to grow. A move was made from their original terminus at Bishopsgate to a newly developed, more spacious site based at Liverpool Street in the City of London. From that time the GER sought to tap the immense and expanding market in people who needed to travel daily by public transport in and out of London and, as a result, the GER become a nationwide leader in the business of carrying passengers the short distances through suburbia. In addition to their preoccupation with passenger transport, the GER was serving agricultural districts and they made every effort to seek the custom of the farmers. In adopting this policy the GER became known as 'the farmer's line' or more affectionately 'the swedey' after the humble root crop grown in many rural districts.

Then, as their routes reached out to the North Sea coastline, it is not surprising that the port of Harwich was targeted for development by the GER, eventually enabling a service to be brought in using their own steamship sailings to and from the Low Countries and Denmark. Eventually Harwich became so busy that a bigger and more convenient replacement port became essential. As a result, Parkeston Quay was developed and took over as the vital point of entry and exit for a vast amount of railway traffic.

The railway made possible the blossoming of the late Victorian enjoyment of day-trips and summer holidays at the seaside, and for the first time the majority of the population could join in the fun. Holiday resorts to cater for the trend sprang up and towns such as Clacton grew in size and popularity.

In the early years of the twentieth century the Great Eastern Railway's management became so skilled at timetabling that the Company ran a suburban passenger service through Essex that was recognized as being the UK's most intensive. Between 1914 and 1918, in addition to major contributions to military transport, one of the greatest areas of support to the Allied cause that the GER in Essex made was in making available Parkeston Quay for use by the Royal Navy.

Post 1918, with the competition on the roads beginning to be serious, it was typical of the efficient strategies of the GER's management that they responded to the situation in a very positive manner, so that by the early 1920s their system of running suburban services in and out of Essex had regained its superiority and once again became a pattern for other railways, worldwide, to follow. The 'Jazz trains', so called from their yellow and blue colour-coded carriage door panels and coloured destination boards, were the pride of the Essex suburban railways until the disruption caused by the General Strike of 1926 became one reason for their disappearance.

In the 1920s little changed on the railways of Essex except the names of the operating companies. The GER became 'grouped' in 1923, joined together with other companies to form the London and North Eastern Railway, but even ten years later the Great Eastern section running was still largely in the hands of ex-GER locomotives with superficial changes only to their livery and numbering. The severe weight restrictions of most routes meant that the Essex main lines were the preserve of such GER passenger classes as Holden's B12 4–6–0s and the smaller 'Claud Hamilton' 4–4–0s. At the same period Holden's 0–6–0T designs along with the J15 0–6–0s and the E4 2–4–0s were the most common motive power on the branchlines. Only when Sir Nigel Gresley's 'Sandringham' B17 4–6–0s and J39 0–6–0s appeared in the mid-1930s did LNER standard designs appear in any quantity and even then the B17s had to be paired with ex–GER tenders to fit on to the turntables of the Essex sheds.

The LNER maintained the company pride that they had inherited in the quality and luxury of the crack expresses, boat trains and Pullman car seaside excursions. The Second World War unravelled many plans to improve the timing of services through Essex along the GER section and it was not until the introduction of the Riddles designed 'Britannia' class 4–6–2 locomotives, starting in 1951 and under the nationalized British Railways (Eastern Region) control, that pre-war passenger timetables could be bettered.

Eleven years after the 'Britannias' and other standard BR steam locomotives were introduced, steam was withdrawn on the GER section of the Essex routes, a time that has been used as a benchmark for this album.

The second company to leave its mark on the railway history of Essex was the London, Tilbury and Southend Railway whose territory was restricted to that southern corridor of Essex that runs parallel to the River Thames, reaching out from Fenchurch Street station in the City of London. The LT&SR originated in 1852 with an Act of Parliament for a joint line owned by the Eastern Counties and London and Blackwall Railways, from Forest Gate Junction on the ECR to Southend via Tilbury. It was originally a 'contractor's line', worked under lease by the contractor who had built the line. In this instance it was Samuel Morton Peto who was joined by Thomas Brassey and E.L. Betts, two other illustrious contractors of the era.

Like its larger neighbour, the LT&SR developed primarily as a 'people carrier' while evolving precocious and ambitious plans for electric motive power as early as 1912. However, electrification had already been achieved in Essex by the London Underground in 1905, with the District Railway reaching Barking by electric traction in April 1908.

The LT&SR had their intentions transferred along with other Company assets when they were taken over, to the surprise of many, by the Midland Railway in 1912. However in spite of directives to the new owners from the Government, plans to electrify the ex–LT&SR lines were finally thwarted by the outbreak of war and steam remained as the motive power on the Tilbury line for many years to follow. The Grouping Act took the MR into the LMS camp. At this stage the enlarged Company made some traffic rearrangements, which led to improved passenger services via LNER-owned Fenchurch Street station with up-to-date carriage stock and Stanier's new taper boilered 2–6–4T design of 1933 specifically targeted for the LT&S section. While the number of boat trains scheduled between St Pancras and Tilbury Docks increased, the few services out of Broad Street to Southend or Tilbury were withdrawn. The District Line electrics, in the meantime, had reached Upminster by 1932.

After the 1948 nationalization the ex-LMS lines in Essex were transferred, with some logic, in 1949, from the London Midland to the Eastern Region of British Railways. Towards the end of steam traction improvements were attempted to what had become, largely as a result of war damage, a run-down passenger service. Newly introduced BR Standard 4MT 2–6–4T locomotives arrived at ex-LT&SR sheds along with better quality BR standard non-corridor carriages. Eventually on both the LT&SR and the GE sections of Essex steam operation ceased in 1962, giving way to electric traction already being established alongside steam services, and by 1967 there was finally the fulfilment of the electrification schemes suggested by the LT&SR fifty-five years previously.

Some independent railway companies, encouraged by the enabling Light Railways Act of 1896, added colourful and slightly eccentric lines to the Essex railway scene. The Corringham Light Railway and the Colne Valley and Halstead were two such which remained viable for relatively long periods. To complete the Essex railway picture independent internal systems also evolved, typified by those particularly associated with the dockland industries along the Essex bank of the Thames estuary. Finally those short lines associated with the seaside, the railway along the pier and the small gauge miniature layout near to the beach, all added variety in times past.

In making this selection of *Essex Railways* and in keeping with the chosen time-span, the boundary of Essex along the Lea Valley relates to the years prior to the formation of the Greater London Council in 1965.

A GER class R24, running as a 2–4–0T, enters the terminus at Tollesbury Pier in pre-grouping days. The siting of the station alongside the River Blackwater did not, however, attract the traffic envisaged. A portion of the pier was removed as an anti-invasion precaution in 1940 and four War Department locomotives, complete with mobile guns, were brought onto the pier section of the branch. Latterly, the stump of the line was used for storing 'cripple' wagons prior to their scrapping. *(Lens of Sutton)*

CHAPTER ONE

WESTERN ESSEX

Burnt Mill station, facing east towards Harlow, opened on 9 April 1841 as Burnt Mill and Netteswell, along with the Northern and Eastern Railway, and closed on 17 July 1960. The platforms were staggered either side of the level-crossing where a crossing-keeper's house (with tall chimney) dates from ECR days. The large timber-built goods shed on the left was reported to have become infested with rats in 1859, so the local ratcatcher-cum-poacher was sent for by the station master. At this, the gamekeeper from the neighbouring estate complained that his sport with terrier dogs would be affected if the rats were totally removed! The stationmaster of the day had already been criticised by the directors for the 'disgusting state of the station lamps and lamp room' and was immediately dismissed from the service of the railway! (Lens of Sutton)

The Main Line

The main line route from London to Cambridge had ancient origins in the proposals as early as 1821 to link the northern coalfields and associated industries through this pathway. Out of these early schemes arose the Northern and Eastern Railway, authorized in 1836 to run from London to Cambridge. Developments were slowed by lack of capital but by 1839 construction had begun, under an agreement, from the Eastern Counties Railway terminus at Shoreditch. The operations had reached Bishop's Stortford by 1843 laying non-standard 5 ft gauge track in order to match the ECR, but there further progress halted. Boardroom rows then led to a change of management personnel and renewed action followed in the form of an Act of Parliament for a northwards extension to Newport, while at the southern end the N&ER claimed to be running the fastest trains in Britain, between Bishop's Stortford and London.

The extension to Newport brought a closer association with the ECR, which culminated in the latter Company leasing the E&R and extending its line through Cambridge to Brandon (by July 1845) to link up with the Norfolk Railway's developing route from Norwich. By this time the E&R had converted their track to standard gauge. This lease continued until the company was bought out by the GER in 1902.

Coal, agricultural produce and general merchandise traffic along the Cambridge route received successive boosts by the opening of the GN&GE Essex Railways Joint Line in 1882, followed by the GER negotiating direct access to the North Derbyshire coalfield through the Lancashire, Derbyshire and East Coast Railway.

Challenge for traffic between the capital and Cambridge came from the Great Northern Railway via their terminus at King's Cross, but by 1905 the GER could not be bettered in its passenger train timing to Cambridge from London. The economic development of the Lea Valley after the First World War maintained the impetus in the line's traffic figures, but in this period it had the image of being less favoured as a route to Norwich. In the early 1930s the Cambridge main-line expresses were still largely made up from the Edwardian era GER coaches, which were lightweight for their capacity, in contrast to the up-to-date LNER Gresley-designed stock used elsewhere on other Essex main lines. This meant that the 'Claud Hamilton' class 4–4–0s were still perfectly adequate to haul thirteen-coach trains from London to Cambridge in the 1930s.

The proximity of important installations made the Cambridge main line very busy during the Second World War when the LNER Thompson B1 class 4–6–0s appeared on the GER section main lines for the first time. However, it was not until the allocation of the BR Standard 'Britannia' class 4–6–2s to Stratford shed for use on the line in 1953 that train timings bettered those of pre-1914 days. Little expenditure on the infrastructure was made before or after the war until the overhead electrification schemes and station refurbishments of the 1960s opened a new era for the Cambridge main line.

The Saffron Walden Railway

With the active backing of the local Gibson family, the Saffron Walden Railway was incorporated in 1865 and opened to Saffron Walden from Audley End on 23 November 1863. The route was extended to the GER station at Bartlow under a second Act of 1863 and opened on 22 October 1866.

The GER, who had put money into the line and worked it from the start, did little to encourage through traffic off the line into Suffolk, and in spite of continued financial input from the Gibsons' own bank the line foundered until bought out by the GER in 1877. Even after this takeover the GER did not develop the possibility of a through route from the Cambridge main line.

After 1923, and the arrival of the LNER, there was no alteration to the basic services of six daily passenger services along the whole route, with additional trains from Saffron Walden to the main line including a through train to Liverpool Street returning from the capital at 6 p.m., hauled by the typical branchline tender engine, the LNER Class E4 2–4–0, members of which had been shedded at Saffron Walden since GER times. As far as locomotive stock is concerned Saffron Walden became well known for the intrusion of GNR locomotives into GER territory when the C12 class 4–4–2T No. 4509 was transferred to Saffron Walden shed in March 1938.

Small industries such as malting and cement offered goods traffic to the line but the Second World War traffic in petroleum for the Walden dump produced a new dimension in traffic. Although the population of the area expanded post war, the old push-and-pull train with its G5 class 0–4–4T was poorly patronized and, in spite of attempts to popularize the single-car diesel units in 1958, the line closed completely on 28 December 1964 following the termination of the passenger service on 7 September of the same year.

The Elsenham to Thaxted Branch

The reputation gained by the GER of being a company that favoured farmers is typified in the branch from Elsenham on the Liverpool Street to Cambridge main line to the town of Thaxted. As its original title, the Elsenham and Thaxted Light Railway, suggests, it was indirectly another product of the 1896 Light Railways Act, although there had been plans prepared for a line from Elsenham beyond Thaxted to Great Bardfield prior to this. Capital proved difficult to raise at the time and it was not until 1906 that a route of just over 5 miles was planned to terminate a mile short of Thaxted. Financial assistance came from the Treasury and also from the GER. Construction started in 1911 and concluded for an opening on 31 March 1913.

There were no signals on the branch, which was worked by one engine in steam with an overall speed limit of 25 mph, reduced to 10 mph over the ungated crossings. Mixed trains were run at times with a guard to collect passsenger fares on the train, using a bell punch to issue bus-type tickets.

Like other lines of similar character, passenger traffic survived to enter British Railways control but only just, closing to passengers on 15 September 1952 and then to freight on 1 June 1953.

Burnt Mill station looking west in LNER days, *c.* 1930s The level-crossing keeper's house dates from the days of the Eastern Counties railway. The signal-box opened in 1881 and closed on 13 June 1960, shortly before the station which was then replaced by Harlow New Town station. *(Lens of Sutton)*

Sawbridgeworth looking south, *c.* 1952. An unidentified ex-LNER Holden J17 0–6–0 running tender first during shunting operations passes (on the right) the original Down platform of *c.* 1841 which was abandoned when the 1865 station was opened. *(D. Lawrence/H. Davies)*

Sawbridgeworth station, built by J. Perry in 1865. The upper view shows the footbridge that was added in 1905, the suggested date of this photograph. Looking towards Bishops Stortford, the shot is taken from the original Downside platform of 1841 when Sawbridgeworth was part of the 5 ft gauge Northern and Eastern Railway. The road forms the county boundary with Hertfordshire, so the signal-box (of 1881) qualifies as being located in Essex. In the lower, older view, the original station building is visible on the left, being retained as accommodation for the stationmaster. The numerous maltings to the west and south of the station created the need for siding space nearby. A small coalyard existed behind the signal-box at a lower level so that coal could be dropped down from above. *(Lens of Sutton)*

Stansted, seen in GER days, looking south with a Down train approaching *c.* 1910. It was opened on 30 July 1845 with the line from Bishop's Stortford to Norwich. The station was rebuilt in 1890, with the platforms being raised over the years to suit the more modern rolling-stock height. The footbridge lasted until electrification in 1987. The signal-box to the right was in use from 1881 to 4 December 1983, having twenty levers expanded to twenty-two when the new goods loop was laid during 1932. *(N. Bowdidge Collection)*

Elsenham station, looking south in 1936, as the Thaxted branch train behind an LNER 0–6–0T enters from the left. In the station is an Up express approaching the photographer. *(Stations UK)*

The view from Elsenham station, looking north, *c.* 1936. The Thaxted branch bay is off the picture to the right. No physical connection existed within the station area, but a spur to the north linked the main line with the LNER goods yard. *(Lens of Sutton)*

Newport signal-box, approved on 28 July 1884, contained a thirty-five lever Saxby frame and lasted until the autumn of 1972 when a raft of runaway wagons demolished the box, resulting in temporary signalling measures being set up in the porter's room. *(Bryan Wilson Collection)*

A GER engineer is taking readings from indicators attached to the locomotive (N31 class No. 999). He is resting against the wooden shelter provided for his protection and is seen through the left-hand cab spectacle on the line between Newport and Elsenham on 22 April 1893. *(Dr Tice Budden courtesy L. Ward and Jack Braithwaite, M&GNR Circle)*

An exterior view of Audley End main station building looking south-west at the north flank elevation 1930s. The building is in almost original condition as when opened with the Eastern Counties line to Brandon. The *porte cochère* was to enable Lord Braybrooke's carriage from Audley End House to be under cover on arrival. The station was built to the design of Francis Thompson between 1844 and 1845, when it was referred to as Wenden station until altered to Audley End on 1 November 1848. *(HMRS/R.Hilton)*

The elegant P43 class 'single' No. 18, heads a train out of Audley End tunnel, *c.* 1905. The form of ballasting seen is typical of the era and a round-ended wagon in the siding to the right is also a period piece. *(HMRS/R. Hilton)*

This Thaxted branch train is leaving Elsenham on 30 June 1951. The connection which was its link to the rest of the railway system was via Elsenham goods yard. The hut in view enclosed the ground frame which operated the points and was released with a key by the train staff. Trains which ran 'mixed' stopped east of the points to attach vehicles from the spur or, on arrival from Thaxted, left them at the frame to be dealt with later after the loco had run round its coaches. Mill Road Halt was just over the brow of the hill in this view. *(H.C. Casserley)*

At Henham Halt, an elderly coach body does service as a shelter on the low platform in typical light railway style, seen just prior to closure in 1952. *(Lens of Sutton)*

Cutlers Green Halt, looking towards Thaxted, with workmen posed to show the finishing touches being completed at the opening of the branch in 1913. The footpath on the left was the only means of access to the low cinder-surfaced platform. *(Stations UK)*

LNER class J69 0–6–0T No. 68530 stands outside Thaxted engine shed on 30 June 1951. The J67, 68 and 69 0–6–0T classes were the mainstay of the motive power for the branch from GER days with only the occasional use of J15 class 0–6–0 tender engines. Repairs and maintenance of the branch loco were carried out at Thaxted's parent Cambridge shed. *(H.C. Casserley)*

LNER class J67/2 0–6–0T No. 68609 waits at Thaxted on 3 June 1951, with the next train to Elsenham. No. 68609 was a regular loco on the branch and one of the type that over the years was converted from J69 to a lower boiler-pressure J67 and back again. The loco shed is to the rear of the train with the 'loco' coalwagon standing on the raised siding, making coaling the loco just a little easier. There was a grounded coach body on the platform as part of the station accommodation. The coaches are converted First World War ambulance vehicles built by the GER. *(H.C. Casserley)*

Class G5 0–4–4T No. 67269 at Audley End, starting away towards Saffron Walden with the 1.55 p.m. push–pull train for Saffron Walden, 28 July 1958. *(Philip J. Kelley)*

Class G5 0–4–4T No. 67279 at Saffron Walden station, 28 July 1956. Auto-driving coach E63423E is paired with non-driving trailer E61441E to make up a push-and-pull train. This coach set was scrapped in 1957. *(Philip J. Kelley)*

Saffron Walden Up starting signal, looking towards Audley End on a white Christmas Day in 1964, three days before official closure although the last freight had run the previous day. *(Bryan Wilson Collection)*

The Great Northern Railway Ivatt-designed class C12 4–4–2Ts had been regular locomotives on the branch since 1938. No. 67375 of that class from Cambridge shed stands taking water on 3 June 1951, while another of the same class is seen beyond the bridge. Nearby, Barnard Bros (corn and seed merchants) had a chute to load their products on to wagons. *(L.R. Peters, courtesy The Gresley Society)*

At Saffron Walden, *c.* 1930, is a fully occupied goods yard with several examples of private-owner wagons, including Saffron Walden Co-op, Charringtons (coal merchants), P.O.P. and J.H. Beattie. To the left of the goods shed is the Railway Hotel to the rear of which were stables for the LNER's working horses. *(Bryan Wilson Collection)*

CHAPTER TWO

THE MAIN LINE FROM LONDON VIA COLCHESTER

Both engine and train are in immaculate condition in this photo. LNER Class B12 4–6–0 No 8552 is pictured heading the Down seven-coach 'Eastern Belle', near Brentwood, c. 1932. This prestigious Pullman train ran between 1929 and 1939 on Sundays to Clacton-on-Sea, but on Mondays to Fridays it was timetabled to a variety of destinations including Felixstowe, Cromer, Sheringham, Lowestoft and even on occasion Skegness and Aldeburgh. Later in its lifetime, in 1939, No. 8852 was one of a few ex-GER locomotives to be transferred to work in Scotland. (R. Carpenter Collection)

The origins of the main line through Colchester lie in the route selected by the Eastern Counties Railway, a company authorized in 1836, which was planned to reach Yarmouth via Colchester, Ipswich, Diss and Norwich but which, by 1843, had managed to finish only the stage to Colchester. The line beyond Colchester had to wait until 1849 for completion, which was by three other companies who arranged for through running to be available.

One of the great selling points for the ECR was the opportunity it would offer farmers to get their products to the London markets in a shorter time and at cheaper rates. 'The greatest livestock line in the kingdom' was how the line was referred to in the 1840s when the first train brought a consignment of sheep from Colchester to Shoreditch and then to Smithfield, on 9 March 1843, twenty days earlier than the first passenger train left Colchester for London.

At the time of the ECR's incorporation, the GWR and I.K. Brunel had opted for their railway to be laid using 7 ft 0¼ in gauge and some of the directors of the ECR wished to follow suit. However the guidance of the ECR's engineer, John Braithwaite, was that the broad gauge would be too expensive and that view prevailed, although with the proviso to rethink it at a later date. Braithwaite then somewhat confused matters, reaching a compromise decision in favour of an entirely unique gauge in the UK of 5 ft, mainly because he considered locomotives could be built with larger and more efficient working parts, thereby creating savings in the long run. Consequently the original line from the London terminus at Shoreditch to Colchester was built to this gauge.

By the autumn of 1843 financial shortfall caused the ECR to abandon its plans for expansion of its main line beyond Colchester to Norwich, and alongside this disappointment came the realization that a 5ft gauge would bring about the same transhipment problems faced by the GWR where contact was to be made with other lines built to the standard gauge. At this stage the ECR directors decided to dispense with the services of the engineer John Braithwaite and replace him with Robert Stephenson, whose known preference was for building railways to the standard 4 ft 8½ in. It was therefore decided to go through the conversion of gauge, work beginning on this on 5 September 1844, which included replacing axles on the current rolling stock as well as relaying track.

The ECR limped on with a poor public image for comfort, speed and punctuality, and the longer route to Norwich via Cambridge was thought to be better than the Colchester main line with its severe speed restrictions at Stratford, Chelmsford and Witham, and with the gradient to climb at Brentwood. The Great Eastern Railway first began running the services on the Colchester main line after an amalgamation between companies that included the ECR, and that happened in 1862. However, it took until the 1870s for improvements to be really noticeable with improved timing and more frequent express services, so that the superiority of the route from London to Norwich via Colchester was regained.

In the 1870s the Colchester main line passed through towns like Ilford and Romford, which were still rural market centres and whose stations dealt with goods and passengers generated by such a hinterland. The growth of market-gardening, fruit-growing and the production of other perishable farm products in the districts alongside the railway through Colchester was greatly assisted by the availability of a quick train service to the London markets, but within twenty years the growth of London's population produced an increased demand for settlement within Essex. There was a need to accommodate the extra suburban passenger flow and, in addition, the increased traffic following the opening of new routes, for example to Clacton and also to Southend. In consequence, a quadrupling of the track from Liverpool Street to Ilford took place in 1895.

In 1914 the American manager of the GER, Henry Thornton, was able to introduce a timetable in which the standard time for all expresses to reach Colchester was 65 minutes (compared to 95 minutes in the summer of 1840 and 130 minutes in 1850). By this time the main line had been quadrupled beyond Ilford to just short of Romford, but war-time conditions prevented any further developments, and by this period road transport was starting to compete seriously with the suburban services on the Colchester main line.

In spite of the growth of the tramways and bus routes, let alone private motoring, congestion on the lines west of Shenfield still presented a problem to management. The LNER had continued to quadruple the main line up to Shenfield by 1934, introducing colour light signalling over the same distance, but in spite of these improvements to the railway infrastructure timings on the main expresses via Colchester were hardly better than in 1914. In contrast more powerful locomotives hauling higher capacity carriages were at work, including rebuilt ex-GER B12 4–6–0s and the new Gresley B17 4–6–0s introduced specifically for use on routes such as the Colchester main line.

Having a garrison town on its route, the Colchester line naturally, as in the First World War, played a significant part in the LNER's invaluable war effort. Five years after the war ended another scheme was introduced to cut the congestion and to improve services for passengers. This was the electrification of the Liverpool Street to Shenfield suburban trains by the overhead system at 1,500V dc, an idea that had surfaced in principle as long ago as 1905, and which probably would have happened earlier if it had not been for the two world wars. In the same period of time work to strengthen bridges and to lift weight restrictions allowed the BR Standard 'Britannia' class 4–6–2s to be introduced and to accelerate the express trains in the Colchester direction out of Liverpool Street, so that Colchester could be reached in 58 minutes by the fastest steam train.

This era was the swan-song of steam as electric traction continued to expand culminating with a change from dc to ac supply over the weekend of 5/6 November 1960. By 1962, with much success in terms of passenger receipts in particular, the whole of the Colchester main line in Essex had been connected up to the overhead system.

Stratford station looking west, with a Down train arriving at the Colchester local platform, *c.* 1910. *(Lens of Sutton)*

A view of Stratford from the low-level station looking north, *c.* 1950. The low-level station was opened in 1854, being served by the Victoria Park to Stratford Bridge trains. The large board on the platform advertises the destinations to be reached from the high-level platforms. The curve to the right is the former Eastern Counties Railway main line. *(Lens of Sutton)*

LNER N7 class 0–6–2T No. 918 rounds the west curve at Stratford on a Woolwich to Fenchurch Street station train, June 1932. *(RAS Marketing)*

This view shows Maryland Point station, which was renamed Maryland on 28 October 1940, looking towards Ilford, *c.* 1940. The steel girders for the new booking hall, spanning the running lines and facing on to Leytonstone Road, can be seen. The station redevelopment was part of the Shenfield electrification scheme, started prior to the Second World War and not completed until 1948. *(Lens of Sutton)*

This scene of Forest Gate shows the entrance to the GER station on the right from street level, *c.* 1910. Pattinson's Toy Bazaar and Dolls Hospital on the left would have been popular with youngsters of the day. The red-brick building, surmounted by a cupola on a corner site, blended the architecture with its select residential image when the station was improved in 1893. At one time Forest Gate booking office claimed the distinction of selling the highest number of season tickets on the GER. *(Lens of Sutton)*

GER class T26 2–4–0 No. 1254 heads a Southend train of four-wheeled coaches between Manor Park and Ilford, 1902. This loco was built in 1902 and survived into BR days (1955). Here it is seen coupled to a 2,790 gallon 'water cart' tender of which ten were surplus to requirement for the 'Claud Hamilton' class and made use of by Stratford works for the final batch of T26s. *(J. Scott-Morgan Collection, courtesy Roger Carpenter)*

Ilford station, looking down Cranbrook Road, is seen here not long after the Ilford Council Tramway had opened in 1905. Ilford was one of the original stations on the first section of the Eastern Counties Railway. It was rebuilt to the style seen here in 1893 and again, but mostly at platform level, in 1898. *(N. Bowdidge Collection)*

Class EB1 Bo–Bo No. 26510, a rebuild by the LNER of a 'one–off', was a design by Sir Vincent Raven. Introduced in 1914 for banking work on the Manchester to Wath line on the North Eastern Railway, this loco is pictured at Ilford car sheds on 28 May 1953 where it had been sent for shunting duties. It was withdrawn in 1964 when the ex–GER lines converted to AC traction. *(Philip J. Kelley)*

Cclass EB1 Bo–Bo No. 26510 at work in Ilford car sheds, 28 May, 1953, hauling a motor coach No. E65245 which had been damaged in a collision with a freight train during the previous week. The coach was being photographed by the official photographer as evidence to be used at an inquiry that was to follow. *(Philip J. Kelley)*

Seven Kings station was opened in March 1899 for passenger traffic when the line was quadrupled through to just short of Romford. This was after 1903 when the Ilford Corporation Tramway from Ilford Broadway to Chadwell Heath was opened. Using raised brickwork on the station name lettering is unusual. *(N. Bowdidge Collection)*

On a typical duty, LNER class D16 4–4–0 No. 8796 hauls a Liverpool Street to Southend express in July 1931 near Chadwell Heath. The lines in the Essex suburbs had been quadrupled by the LNER by this date. *(RAS/Photomatic)*

Romford Factory, Gidea Park, was the site of the original Eastern Counties Railway works before the opening of Stratford Works in 1848. When this view was taken, on 9 May 1955, the building was in use producing wagon sheets. *(Philip J. Kelley)*

LNER class D15 4–4–0 No. 8821 heads a down Walton-on-the-Naze express from Liverpool Street past Romford in August 1931. *(RAS/Photomatic)*

LNER class B17/2 4–6–0 No. 2811 *Raynham Hall* near Romford on a Down express, in August 1931, when the locomotive was just one year old. This engine is fitted with a Westinghouse pump on the side of the boiler as part of the air-braking system. Behind the engine is a short GER-type tender. *(RAS/Photomatic)*

These two views show the GER station at Romford, *c.* 1910. Above, is a GER 2–4–0 at the head of a train in the Down platform, while below, the photographer is looking in the opposite direction, to the west. The LNER widened the route from Liverpool Street station to Shenfield to four lines in the early 1930s and Romford station was reconstructed at that time. The inclined footways on either side of the station platforms gave access to the town below the embankment. The footbridge seen in the top view provided a link with the adjacent LT&SR station. *(Lens of Sutton)*

This scene shows Romford Factory, 1 June 1911, looking towards London from Factory signal-box. In front of the Provender store, built 1902, are sheeted wagons loaded with hay ready to supply the needs of some of the many horses working within the GER system at the time. The building also housed the GER's clock-repair depot. A 2–4–2T stands in the carriage sidings to the right. *(HMRS/R. Hilton)*

Romford station looking towards the down side-entrance with the motor-vehicle starting to infiltrate the taxi-ranks, *c.* 1911. The motor-car on the right stands alongside the Star Hotel (out of view), and probably the star on its radiator signifies its ownership. *(N. Bowdidge Collection)*

Here, an outer suburban train is seen at Gidea Park station, *c.* 1922. The GER C32 class 2–4–2T No. 1075 was not built with a condenser, unlike twenty of its sister engines. A stovepipe chimney was typical at the time, as was the livery of grey with large numerals on the tankside. *(Lens of Sutton)*

The GER class T19 2–4–0 Large Boiler No. 1034, nicknamed 'Humpty Dumpties', passes Harold Wood station, on 18 August 1908, with the 1.45 p.m. Liverpool Street to Norwich express. *(LCGB/K. Nunn)*

This view from the early 1900s shows a Down train arriving at Brentwood. The number of passengers waiting suggests that it might be an excursion. The locomotive is a T26 class 2–4–0. To the left at the far end of the Up platform can be seen the old bell tower, which was demolished in the 1930s when the line was quadrupled. The station signal-box appears to the right of the train. *(N. Bowdidge Collection)*

For many years Brentwood was a garrison town, with army barracks at Warley. There was a bay platform in the distance (behind the marching soldiers), which was much used for military traffic. The crowd here had stopped to watch the 1st Norfolk Regiment leave in 1909. *(N. Bowdidge Collection)*

Immaculately polished GER class D56 4–4–0 No. 1829, conveying King George V and his entourage to Sandringham, passes Brentwood on 28 June 1911. The locomotive is displaying the four-disc headcode reserved for a royal train. *(LCGB/K. Nunn)*

GER class D56 4–4–0 No. 1855, the 3.30 p.m. Ipswich to Liverpool Street mails, collects a mail bag on the move from lineside equipment that can be seen to the right of the first vehicle, 11 August 1908. *(LCGB/K. Nunn)*

LNER class D15 4–4–0 No. 8832 ascends Brentwood Bank with a Down express. The scene dates from a time before August 1930 when No. 8832 was rebuilt with a round-topped boiler, becoming Class B12/3. *(RAS Marketing)*

Ex-LNER class Y11 petrol 0–4–0 No. 15098 was built by the Motor Rail Tramcar Co., Bedford (Simplex), Works No. 1931, and known locally either as *The Greenhouse*, or *Peggy*, after the horse it supplanted. It is seen here at Brentwood yard on 3 September 1953. When bought by the LNER in 1925 it was renumbered 8430. The driving wheels were only 3 ft 1 in in diameter. *(Philip J. Kelley)*

Another view of ex-LNER class Y11 0–4–0, in April 1949, shows its last LNER number still on display. Brentwood Yard forms the background, with the coal merchant's name prominent. *(RAS/Photomatic)*

An unidentified GER 4–4–0 class S46 'Claud Hamilton' 4–4–0 on an Up train, enters Brentwood station, *c.* 1911. The loading dock, specifically for military personnel and equipment, is seen behind the station railings. *(HMRS/R. Hilton)*

GER Holden class T26 2–4–0 hauls a St Pancras to Clacton excursion train past Brentwood yard signal-box on 3 April 1909. Between 1891 and 1902 100 of this class were built at Stratford works. Here, No. 1257 has a boiler with a dome on the front ring. Built in 1902, No. 1257 survived to be scrapped in 1957 as BR No. 62796. *(LCGB/K. Nunn)*

Seen here at Brentwood station are the station staff and constable, for which a date of around 1860 has been suggested. The gentleman next to the policeman is said to be Porter Hunnikin and, next to him, Foreman Porter Ninett. *(N. Bowdidge Collection)*

GER class S46 4–4–0 No. 1870 passes Ingrave signal-box on Brentwood Bank on 6 July 1912. A mixture of non–passenger rolling stock makes up the 1.00 p.m. Marks Tey to Bishopsgate 'Green Pea' special. This train made express deliveries of the green pea harvest from market gardens in Essex to the London markets. *(LCGB/K.Nunn)*

The original road frontage of the Shenfield and Hutton Junction station with the station staff and some local people standing outside the stationmaster's house, early 1900s. The station entrance is to the left of the house. Through the bridge is the road to Billericay and above the bridge is a fine example of a GER junction signal arrangement with repeating arms low on the post. The signal controls the junction to Southend and the Colchester main line. *(N. Bowdidge Collection)*

A view of Shenfield station showing two porters and a railway clerk at the London end of the platforms, *c.* 1905. Milk churns by the foot crossing demonstrate an item of the rural goods traffic of the day. *(N. Bowdidge Collection)*

GER Class N31 0–6–0 No. 550 approaches Shenfield with a Spitalfields to Parkeston Quay special goods train, 7 June 1908. *(LCGB/K. Nunn)*

A GER class T26 2–4–0 heads the 3.27 p.m. Liverpool Street to Southend train near Shenfield on 5 April 1913. *(LCGB/K. Nunn)*

The 6.40 p.m. Liverpool Street to Norwich, 'The East Anglian', near Shenfield on 10 June 1938. In the fashion of the day, two 'Sandringham' 4–6–0s were streamlined at Doncaster by the LNER in 1937 especially to work this express. They became Class B17/5 and the engine seen here, No. 2870, was renamed *City of London* in exchange for *Manchester City* in the process. By the end of May the two streamlined 'Sandringhams' had been responsible for 328 double trips, and both engines had completed 40,000 miles each by June 1938. *(LCGB/K. Nunn)*

BR class 7MT Standard 4–6–2 No. 70010 *Owen Glendower* on the London-bound 'Norfolkman' express (5.45 p.m. from Norwich), approaching Shenfield on 9 July 1955. The 'Norfolkman' began running as a named train in 1948. The introduction of the 'Britannia' class enabled this train to be accelerated to 2 hours 10 minutes for the journey from Norwich to Liverpool Street, with a stop at Ipswich. *(Philip J. Kelley)*

The second LNER streamlined B17/5 class No. 2859 *East Anglian* hauls the Up train of the same name past Goodmayes on 28 September 1937, the second day of the service. *(LCGB/K. Nunn)*

GER class T 19R 4–4–0 No. 1035 stands at Chelmsford on 15 June 1907. The brass numberplate is typical of the period, while the locomotive has entered service in the grey livery which was the custom of the day when a works photograph was required. The engines so treated were nicknamed 'Dolly Grey' after a Boer War period popular song. *(LCGB/K. Nunn)*

GER class S46 4–4–0 No. 1878 passes over Chelmsford Viaduct with the 1.50 p.m. Lowestoft to Liverpool Street express on 8 September 1911. *(LCGB/K. Nunn)*

GER class S46 4–4–0 No. 1864 hauls a long train of empty wagons from Temple Mills goods yard to Lowestoft near Chelmsford on 15 October 1913. *(LCGB/K. Nunn)*

Thompson class B1 4–6–0 No. 61045 on 'East Anglian' duty and in early BR livery heads the Up 11.40 a.m. Norwich–Liverpool Street express near Chelmsford on 10 September 1949. *(LCGB/K. Nunn)*

In this view of Chelmsford station, looking towards Colchester, *c.* 1910, the signal-box and high-level goods shed can both be seen above the canopy of the Down platform. The station area nearest to the viewer is supported on a viaduct. Originally the station existed as an island platform until rebuilt in 1856 to the form depicted. *(N. Bowdidge Collection)*

GER class N31 0–6–0 No. 935, trundles out of Colchester hauling a long string of wagons making up the 11 a.m. Clacton goods, 22 March 1913. *(LCGB/K. Nunn)*

GER Class C53 No. 126 travelling light engine, is seen here near Colchester at 5.30 a.m., 13 March 1921, on its way from Stratford works to Ipswich. The date suggests that it is brand new and it appears that grey has replaced the blue, lined red livery below the wooden body. The tram engines were always closely associated with the Wisbech and Upwell Tramway and of course were immortalized by the Revd Wilbert Awdry as 'Toby the Tram Engine'. *(LCGB/K. Nunn)*

One of many troop specials helping to mobilize troops in August 1914 is seen in this view headed by GER class T26 2–4–0 No. 1250, 16 August 1914. It was on the first part of a journey from St Botolph's, Colchester, to embark the men at Plymouth Docks. *(LCGB/K. Nunn)*

GER Holden class T26 2–4–0 stands in Colchester station with a stopping train on 15 November 1911. *(Lens of Sutton)*

The derailed restaurant cars of the Up Cromer express whose locomotive GER class S69 No. 1506 collided with a light engine at the west end of Colchester station (class T26 No. 471) on Saturday 12 July 1913. The driver and fireman of the express, William Barnard and Sidney Keeble, were killed instantly and the guard, George Burdett, died shortly afterwards. *(LCGB/K. Nunn)*

GER class T19R 4–4–0 No. 741 at Colchester on 13 March 1921. This locomotive was rebuilt from James Holden's class T19 2–4–0. *(LCGB/K. Nunn)*

A general view of Colchester station, *c.* 1900, during the rebuilding and extension of the Down platform, so the view is towards London. The Clacton bay is to the left and an engine inspection pit, water column and loco sandbox are at the country end of the platform. *(HMRS/R. Hilton)*

A more distant view of the eastern end of Colchester station, *c.* 1910, with a GER 4–4–0 signalled to depart from the Down platform. The Clacton Bay is to the left. To the left again is the former Victoria Hotel, opened in 1843. Many changes to this view have taken place, not least those associated with the reconstruction work in conjunction with the electrification scheme begun in early 1960 and completed by 1962. *(Lens of Sutton)*

An early view, *c.* 1875, of the eastern end of Colchester station, taken from the windows of the Essex Hall Asylum, formerly the Victoria Hotel. A GER Sinclair 2–4–0 design coupled to a passenger brake van stands in the platform. The large building on the right is a public house. *(HMRS/R. Hilton)*

Colchester station, *c.* 1910, looking east, with a view of the canopy of the Up platform which has by this time been extended to include the Clacton Bay platform where a locomotive can be glimpsed. *(Lens of Sutton)*

Colchester steam shed looking towards Ipswich, was built in 1890 and was still in operation, in about 1955, when this photograph was taken. The grounded body served as a messroom until a prefabricated building was put up in 1956. The chimney seen above the cab of ex-LNER class J15 0–6–0 No. 65465 shows the position of the shedmaster's office. The through shed replaced the original Eastern Counties Railway construction. *(R. Carpenter Collection)*

Colchester shed's own class B17/4 4–6–0 *The Essex Regiment* rests at home on 8 April 1956. Originally named *Newcastle United*, it was renamed in June 1936 to honour the county regiment. It was withdrawn from Stratford shed in December 1959. *(F.M. Wycherley)*

This view of the original Eastern Counties Railway station is thought to show the Colchester station that was rebuilt in about 1900. *(N. Bowdidge Collection)*

An overall view of the western approaches to Colchester shows the snow of January 1960. The marshalling yard in the middle ground is in front of the tranship shed and to the rear is the chimney of the railway's laundry and a water tower. On the skyline to the right is the former ECR Victoria Hotel. *(HMRS)*

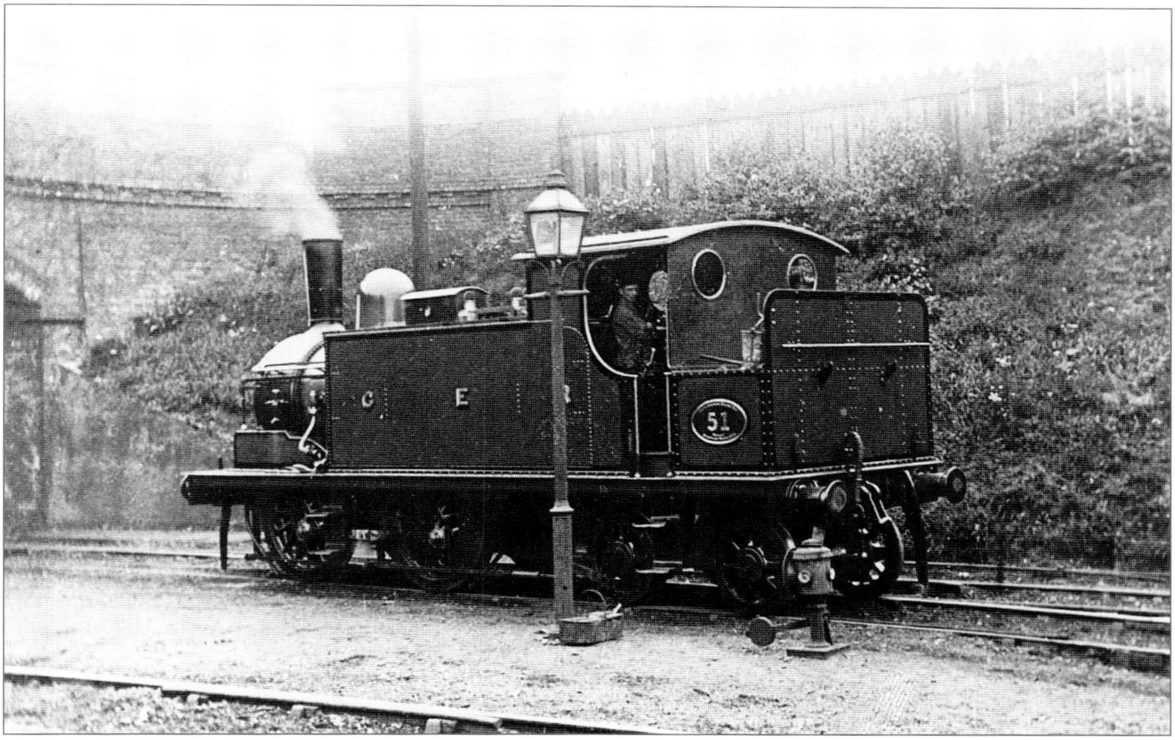

Bromley E10 class 0–4–4T No. 51, rebuilt with rear cab protection for the footplate crew in 1892, is seen here in Witham in the 1890s. Later, coalrails were fitted around the bunker to increase coal-carrying capacity. *(Photomatic/M&GN Circle)*

Witham station, looking north-east, is seen here in the aftermath of the wreck of the Cromer express on 1 September 1905. *(A. Corder-Birch Collection)*

In this view of Marks Tey looking west towards Kelvedon, *c.* 1900, the main station building can be seen on the left, and a Down train stands at the platform. A passenger train headed by a tank engine stands in the Stour Valley platform, while a goods for that line is headed by a GER class Y14 0–6–0. Watering facilities are available alongside the timber goods shed. *(HMRS/R. Hilton)*

Holden's class B12 4–4–0 LNER No. 8568 approaches Manningtree on an Up slow train across the north junction with the Harwich line, *c.* 1931. The experimental energy-conserving apparatus, including two cylindrical tanks on the boiler top, equated to rucksacks worn by the ramblers of the day, causing these engines to become nicknamed 'Hikers'. *(RAS/Photomatic)*

Chapter Three

The Essex Suburbs from Liverpool Street

Loughton New Station looking towards Epping, 1948. The Joint London Transport and LNER 1935–40 New Works Programme had advocated electrification of the Loughton Branch and Fairlop loop, and their connection to the Underground system via an extension of the Central line beyond Liverpool Street station. With the war intervening the work had only reached Loughton in 1948, although the new station had been in use since 1940. In this view the centre station road was not electrified, being reserved for the steam push-and-pull service to Ongar. Steam was eventually displaced from Loughton station when electrified traction was phased in throughout the branch in 1957. (Philip J. Kelley)

In 1862 the Great Eastern Railway sought Parliamentary powers to build a railway that would tap into the popularity of the 'day out' to Epping Forest, an excursion that had become so popular among East End Londoners in particular. The Chingford branchline was authorized on 23 June 1864 from the GER's Loughton branch near the junction with the Cambridge line, through Walthamstow (Wood Street) and ¾-mile beyond Chingford to High Beech in Epping Forest. Soon after, on 29 July 1864, the GER was granted powers to build Liverpool Street station and the lines to Hackney Downs. From there the line was to divide, one section linking to Edmonton and the other to Wood Street and High Beech with two spurs to the Cambridge line. Financial difficulties meant very little work was completed and led to the abandonment of the original permission in exchange for new powers to continue from the already completed Hackney Downs to Walthamstow extension as far as Chingford only. A spur was to connect the Cambridge main line with the Walthamstow branch at Lea Bridge Junction.

The terminus at Chingford, intended as a temporary measure only, was completed in November 1873, when the passenger service was worked into Bishopsgate (low level) prior to transfer to the new Liverpool Street station on 2 February 1874. A much larger terminus was opened at Chingford on 2 September 1878 and with its growing traffic another abortive attempt was made to continue the route into the heart of Epping Forest. The Chingford branch was doubled by September 1878, with the old station layout put to use as part of the goods yard. Yet another attempt was made in 1882 to extend the line into the Forest from Chingford, but again without success. An extension to the passenger service along the Tottenham and Hampstead Railway to Highgate Road and then to Gospel Oak occurred in 1885. Other developments, one involving electric traction, were planned as the districts around Walthamstow mushroomed with new houses.

At the time of the First World War Armistice the Chingford line returned to its earlier levels of passenger traffic – on Whit Monday 1920, 100,000 passengers arrived at Chingford – and in 1920 the intensive passenger timetable working referred to as the 'Jazz Service' was in operation on the line. The GER considered the possibility of reaching Ongar via the much-proposed High Beech extension and a junction on the Ongar line at High Weald, but nothing materialized. Services were mainly in the hands of tank locomotives of the G4 0–4–4T and J69 0–6–0T types in the inter-war years when passenger services retained their volume, and resignalling of the line with searchlight colour signals was brought into use on 29 January 1938. Cuts in passenger services made during the Second World War were never reinstated and the branch went into a decline, partly due to competition from London Underground trains. Overhead electrification on the ac system was inaugurated on 14 November 1960, when electric trains first ran in public service on the Chingford line.

The Fairlop Loop

Opened by the GER on 1 May 1903, the line made a triangular junction between Ilford and Seven Kings stations on the Romford line and ran 6¼ miles north, turning west near Grange Hill station to meet the Loughton and Ongar line with a south-facing junction north of Woodford station. There was less housing development than had been anticipated close to the loop line stations north of Barkingside in the years before the First World War and Hainault station was closed to all traffic, but not dismantled, on 1 October 1908, and later reopened for passenger traffic only on 3 March 1930. Barkingside was closed to passengers on 22 May 1916 then re–opened on 1 July 1919.

The steam service was withdrawn on 30 November 1947 and replaced by LPTB buses carrying special destination indicators, 'Railway Service–Woodford–All Stations'. Last train ceremonies were held on 29 November 1947, class N7 0–6–2Ts Nos 9732 and 9645 being the locomotives involved, and hauling the final services from Ilford and Woodford respectively.

The Fairlop loop was reopened to the Central line tube train service after the steam service was withdrawn. This event took place between Newbury Park and Hainault on 31 May 1948, and extended to Woodford on 21 November 1948, the same day that the tube reached Loughton.

The Ongar Branch

In 1856 the Eastern Counties Railway opened a double-track branch to Loughton and a single-line continuation through to Epping. This was then extended to Ongar in 1865. The opening of the Fairlop Loop in 1903 spread wider the dense network of short branchlines in south-west Essex, attempting to cope with the demand for public transport that the suburban sprawl was causing. However, this caused even more congestion and securing pathways for express services in and out of Liverpool Street station became a major headache. The GER addressed the problem, but were frustrated by financial restrictions and, similarly, the London Underground Group was unable to proceed with plans for an extension of its lines into the area.

Eventually, in 1935, the joint London Transport and LNER New Works programme advocated electrification and connection to the Underground system as the answer to the problems. The year 1940 was the time that the enabling Act of 1936 had set to see electrified services start. Problems with the Parliamentary insistence on an alteration of the existing road bridges, rather than their replacement by level-crossings at many sites, meant that little work was done before the war finally stopped progress altogether. The line to Loughton was eventually electrified in 1948, followed by an extension to Epping on 25 September 1949.

Poor returns resulted from decreased traffic and in 1952 a lightweight diesel unit was operated under trial conditions. Failure of these units to match expectations caused other action to be considered and, although closure was ruled out at this stage, diesel haulage replaced steam on goods traffic and then, on 18 November 1957, Central Line trains extended their journey to terminate at Ongar. Goods services were withdrawn in the mid-1960s and Leyton Junction was lifted in 1972, thereby isolating the Ongar line from the rest of BR(E). Total closure followed in 1995, only for the line to live on in part as a preservation project.

Highams Park looking towards Chingford from the level-crossing, *c.* 1910. It was opened with the line from Wood Street (Shern Hall Street) to Chingford Green and, originally named Hale End on 17 November 1873, it was regarded by the GER as a temporary arrangement. However, local people petitioned the Company to make the station permanent, which they did, also doubling the track and providing a Down platform. The Mackenzie and Holland signal-box was replaced in 1926 and resited. The signal-post has a repeater arm to allow visibility below the station awning. *(Lens of Sutton)*

The exterior of Chingford station, *c.* 1905, showing the style of architecture adopted by the GER in the Essex suburbs. This building replaced a timber single-storey structure in 1878. Chingford witnessed the Royal Train in 1882 with a GER loco painted royal blue for the occasion, said to be the origin of the smart GER livery of the following decades. The famous 'Jazz Train' service started to Chingford in 1920 with its colour-coded destination panels on the carriage doors. *(N. Bowdidge Collection)*

The G4 0–4–4Ts were regular performers on the Chingford branch during the 1920s. In this view No. 8126 is arriving with a Down train from Liverpool Street while No. 1123 stands in the engine siding awaiting its next turn of duty, 9 June 1924. *(GERS Collection of Historical Records and Relics)*

Walthamstow, Hoe Street station was the venue for an LNER open day exhibition on 29 and 30 May 1937 as part of a public relations exercise. Among the locomotives on view was Gresley A4 Pacific 4–6–2 No. 4482 *Golden Eagle*. *(GERS Collection of Historical Records and Relics)*

Loughton Branch Junction signal-box, 14 October 1954. It is supported by timbers following subsidence caused during construction of London Transport, Central Line tube tunnels between Stratford and Leyton. *(Philip J. Kelley)*

Leyton (Low Leyton until 27 November 1867) is seen here with what looks like an excursion train expected, as 'couples', the ladies in their best hats, wait on the platform. High Road bridge at the south end was the main entrance from 1879, with another entrance and exit being provided at the opposite end in 1901. *(Lens of Sutton)*

Leytonstone station is seen here looking towards Leyton, with a GER tank locomotive entering the Down platform with an Epping train. The wartime bombing in 1944 and the electrification plans of London Transport caused the demolition of the station buildings and the addition of a third platform positioned on the site of the main station building. *(Lens of Sutton)*

This view shows Leytonstone station entrance, *c.* 1910. This was the second station out from Stratford on the 1856 Loughton Branch of the Eastern Counties Railway. A GER horse-van stands in the forecourt in front of the mock Tudor-style building, a replacement of an earlier building by contractor A.J. Bateman in 1891–2. The stationmaster's house is to the left and coal merchant C.W. Tanner has an office to the right. *(Lens of Sutton)*

This scene of Snaresbrook and Wanstead station looking north, *c.* 1910, shows the starting signal with the Eagle Lane distant arm underneath. The signals are repeated above for the driver's better view over the platform canopy. The station opened on 22 August 1856 as Snaresbrook, Wanstead being added in November 1898. It reverted at the time of Underground electrification in December 1947. *(Lens of Sutton)*

A reversal of the station name appears on this postcard, which is looking south with a Down train approaching, *c.* 1910. By this period an additional Down side bay was provided for terminating passenger services. The disc in the foreground is the signal for the cross-over points. *(Lens of Sutton)*

This view shows George Lane station and level-crossing looking south-east, *c.* 1905. The station opened with the line to Loughton on 22 August 1856 and was renamed South Woodford (George Lane) on 5 July 1937, to become plain Woodford with electrification in 1947 when the level-crossing was removed. *(Lens of Sutton)*

In this scene of George Lane looking north, *c.* 1910, the lady reads while waiting for her London-bound train. In the background is the weatherproof footbridge and the level-crossing. The elegant lamp-post provided for illumination by gas. *(Lens of Sutton)*

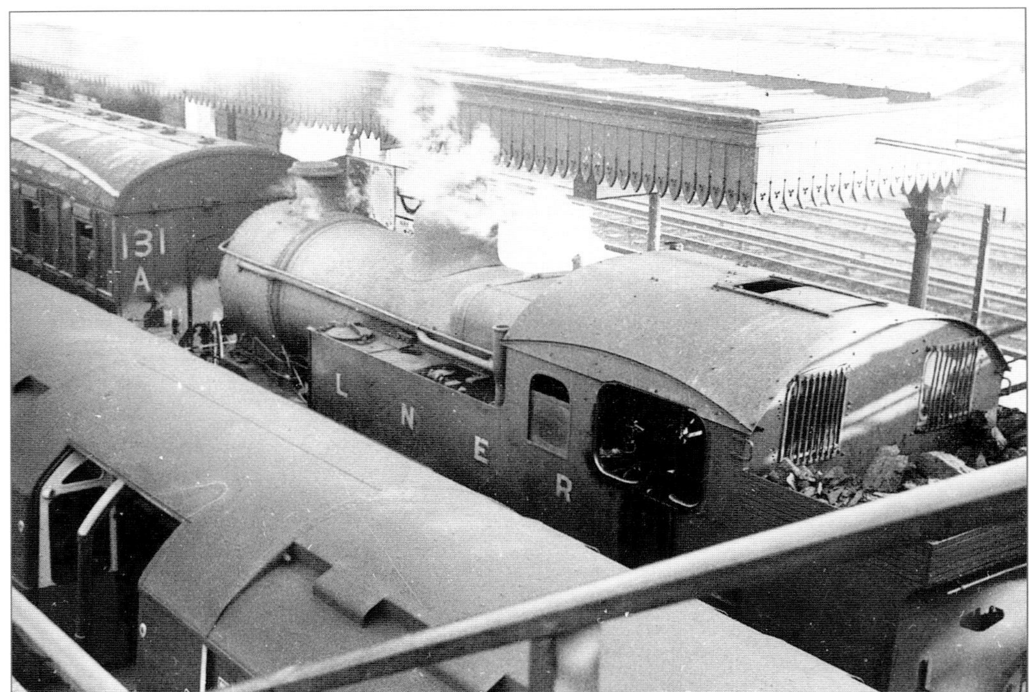

An unidentified class N7 0–6–2T at Woodford station, with a tube train in the foreground, travels on the last day of steam services on 21 October 1948. Steam trains shuttled between Leytonstone and Ongar until 14 December 1947 when they were cut back to Woodford. *(Philip J. Kelley)*

Class F5 2–4–2T No. 67203 at Woodford, on 21 October 1948, was carrying passengers on the last day of steam services to Woodford. London Transport tube trains ran through to Loughton after this date, and No. 67203 was converted for push-and-pull working in 1949. *(Philip J. Kelley)*

Stationmaster Grantham (left) retired on 21 October 1948, the day that London Transport took over the running of Woodford station. The replacement stationmaster alongside Mr Grantham wears the cap badge of the new management. *(Philip J. Kelley)*

An excursion train to Clacton, hauled by class N7/5 0–6–2T No. 69630, leaves South Woodford on 7 July 1957. Steam haulage on the line continued to be used on such services, as well as goods trains which shunted the small yards, such as the one in view, which was then still open for business. *(Philip J. Kelley)*

This scene shows Loughton station approach and loading dock, looking north-east from the station in 1911. An 0–6–0T stands awaiting its next duty opposite the neat allotments on the embankment. The building nearest the camera on the left is a stable. *(HMRS/R. Hilton Collection)*

The Eastern Counties Railway opened the double track branch to Loughton in 1856. This view of Loughton, *c.* 1900, is looking across the access road to the station entrance. The sign on the right between the two sets of close-coupled carriages reads 'J & H Girling, Coal Merchants'. *(HMRS/R. Hilton Collection)*

Class N7/1 0–6–2T No. 9645 on an Up train passing Theydon Bois signal-box on 13 September 1948. The scene is prior to electrification as it was not until 25 September 1949 that tube services reached Epping. *(Philip J. Kelley)*

In this view of Epping station in 1957 a southbound LT Central Line train is dwarfed by a class F5 2–4–2T No. 67202 of Stratford shed on a push-and-pull train heading in the opposite direction. The tripcock for safe running over electrified lines can be seen below the bufferbeam of the train engine. *(D. Lawrence via Hugh Davies)*

A distant view of Epping station looking north, *c.* 1903, showing Epping gas works with its own siding to the right and the goods yard to the left. The double line reverted to single from here onwards to Ongar. The engine in view is GER class C32 2–4–2T No. 1041. *(HMRS/R. Hilton)*

Class F5 2–4–2T No. 67193 leaves North Weald station for Epping, on 28 April 1948. The aerials in the background are reminders of the fighter station and its associations with the Battle of Britain squadrons. This was a push-and-pull service with the loco at the Epping end, as was the custom dictated by facilities in Epping yard. *(Philip J. Kelley)*

The gradient post at North Weald, the highest point on the ex-GER, was 340 ft above sea level, and is seen here on 24 June 1950. *(LCGB/K. Nunn)*

Class J15 0–6–0 No. 65463, brings the 5.19 p.m. passenger train from Ongar to Epping into Blake Hall, Saturday 20 September 1952. All passenger trains were strengthened on that day in connection with an RAF display at North Weald aerodrome, commemorating the twelfth anniversary of the Battle of Britain. This loco, and another of the same class (No. 65450) were brought specially from Stratford shed to cope with the traffic. There is evidence below the buffer beam of the locomotive of the conductor rails set up in readiness for the aborted electrification plan of 1940. *(Philip J. Kelley)*

Ongar station and signal-box, seen on 28 April 1956, looking towards the buffer stops with class F6 2–4–2T No. 67183 on an Epping train. The branch from Epping to Ongar was handed over to the control of London Transport in 1950 when electrification reached Epping, but the goods yards to the right and left of this view were retained by the Eastern Region of British Railways until closure in 1966. *(Philip J. Kelley)*

This view of Barkingside station, looking south, shows the cupola on the Down platform station building that placed the style of the station architecture of this station above the general distinction of the other Fairlop loop line stations. As a part of the railway economy policy during the First World War, Barkingside station was closed to passenger traffic on 22 May 1916 until 1 July 1919. The station served the Dr Barnardo's Village Home for Girls and in this view his funeral cortège is under way, with a large number of mourners in attendance. *(Lens of Sutton)*

Hainault station, seen here looking towards Fairlop, was a station that opened on 1 May 1903 but closed soon after on 1 October 1908 as the anticipated housing development had not materialized. It reopened on 3 March 1930, having been available a few years before workmen and others wanting tickets on advance application. The BR service was withdrawn on 31 May 1948 when the LT Central Line trains were extended to Newbury Park. *(Lens of Sutton)*

Two comparable views show the exterior of Chigwell station. In GER days, *c.* 1900, the horse predominates (above) but by about 1930 the small private saloon car appears, parked outside a branch of Barclays Bank (below). Chigwell was the only station on the Fairlop line which served a sizeable local village, but because of its situation between a cutting on the Grange Hill side and a large embankment in the Woodford direction there was no room for a goods yard. *(Lens of Sutton)*

CHAPTER FOUR

SOUTH-EAST ESSEX & THAMESIDE

Shoeburyness station in the heyday of the LMS Stanier three-cylinder 2–6–4Ts, is seen here on 27 June 1936, with a two-year-old No. 2508 waiting to leave platform 2 with a set of much older ex-Midland Railway, Clayton designed flat-roofed suburban stock, bound, as the destination board announces, for Fenchurch Street station. These boards were a feature on passenger trains until phased out when the Eastern Region of BR took control of the line in 1949. Beyond the locomotive is Shoeburyness running shed which, along with Plaistow, Tilbury, Upminster and Devons Road, Bow serviced the locomotive stock of the section. (Lens of Sutton)

The London Tilbury and Southend Railway

This railway developed from a line jointly owned by the Eastern Counties and the London and Blackwall Railway, from Forest Gate Junction on the ECR to Southend via Tilbury. The Act for this line was passed in 1852, and on 13 April 1854 some 17 miles of track were opened from Forest Gate to Tilbury. This line was named the London, Tilbury and Southend Extension Railway. A branch to Thames Haven was opened later, in 1855, having been taken over by the LTSR from its independent builders, the Thames Haven Dock and Railway Company.

Initially Tilbury trains were sorted into Bishopsgate and Fenchurch Street portions at Stratford, a practice which soon became unwieldy and a direct route through Plaistow from Fenchurch Street station was constructed and opened in 1858. The Tilbury system took over an earlier proposed Tilbury–Pitsea line in 1855 before the main Tilbury line had reached Leigh on Sea.

The contracting firm of Peto, Brassey and Betts leased the running of the line at its opening and they in turn handed the running over to the Eastern Counties Railway. Efforts to transfer the Tilbury to the GER when the ECR's lease ran out in 1875 were resisted and a period followed when rolling stock was borrowed from the GER, until 1880, by which time the newly incorporated London Tilbury and Southend Railway had taken delivery of its own stock, including its first 4–4–2T locomotives.

The Barking–Upminster–Pitsea direct line was opened in stages from 1883 to 1888, the Shoeburyness extension in 1884, followed by a link with the original route by the single-line Upminster–Grays route in 1892. The latter pushed north to Romford in the following year.

The LT&SR developed a massive market in commuters, coastal seaside excursions and the Tilbury port traffic, and became a target for takeover from both the GER and Midland Railway Directors. Against expectations, the Midland Railway achieved this objective and absorbed the LTSR in 1912, with proposals for a radical electrification scheme at the time. The onset of the First World War put an end to this scheme and then, in 1922, the LMS became responsible for the running of the line. The LMS introduced through trains between Broad Street and Southend in 1925, and new stations for use by District Line electrics which were provided with extra tracks. Further attempts to upgrade the line were made when the newly designed Stanier 2–6–4Ts were introduced to the line in 1934, along with improved carriage stock.

In BR days the line was transferred from the London Midland to Eastern Region in 1949, when integration into the ER electrification programme took place, only for this to undergo further delay while the technical problems of electrification were sorted out.

Thameside Industries

The east of the confluence of the Rivers Lea and Thames, throughout Thameside, has seen the development of a number of independent railway systems, the Victoria Dock of 1855 being the first dock in the world designed to include an integrated railway system. With the opening of the Royal Albert Dock in 1880, the owning dock company built a passenger railway which connected with the GER at Custom

House station. In 1909 the newly created Port of London Authority inherited the former dock companies' intricate railway systems, which they ran until the early 1970s, by which time containerization brought a change in transport requirements from those of the 1960s.

The Gas Light and Coke Co.'s Beckton gas works of 1870, north of Gallions Reach, built its own railway to Custom House in 1871, leasing it to the GER from 1874. Passenger services were run until 1940, entirely for the benefit of the workforce. The internal system at Beckton became well known for its eccentric looking 'cut down' locomotives, designed to enable passage under the low entrances to the retort houses, and this internal railway continued in use until 1971 when the supply of North Sea natural gas took the place of coal gas. In addition, other industrial railway complexes such as that constructed by Ford's of Dagenham, or the purely internal lines of the Shoeburyness Garrison Railway, were part of the Thameside railway scene.

Shenfield to Southend

The GER received Parliamentary permission to build a line from Shenfield to Southend, a distance of 21¼ miles, on 16 July 1883. The line opened in piecemeal fashion, first to Wickford for goods in 1888, then on New Year's Day 1889 passengers could travel to Wickford. Later that year the total length to Southend opened on 1 October. The single line was doubled in 1901, as traffic demands increased, with the excursion trains in the forefront. Stations were provided at Billericay, Rayleigh and Hockley to cater for the increase in the local population.

On 11 June 1956 the 1,500V dc suburban overhead electrification scheme included the Shenfield to Southend line in its plan of where electrification should be extended on 31 December 1956. The dc system was converted to ac in November 1961.

At Southend-on-Sea, 'For Westcliffe and Thorpe Bay', a Holden GER class D56 4–4–0 waits on platform 4, *c.* 1910, with a departure facing London. *(Lens of Sutton)*

The Corringham Light Railway

The 2¾-mile long railway between Corringham and Coryton (formerly Kynochtown) was another product of the 1896 Light Railway Act, the promoters having obtained a Light Railway Order in 1899. Built to serve Kynoch's (Birmingham) new explosives factory, the line was opened for goods on 1 January 1901 and then for passengers on 22 June 1901. In addition to the main route, a siding connection was put in to the LT&SR's Thames Haven branch.

The demands of the First World War propelled the Light Railway into vastly increased activity, both in passenger and goods traffic, causing the management to provide itself with two extra locomotives and ten more bogie carriages. Considering its main function was to move ammunition, it is surprising that the line did not come under wartime Government control as did most other companies in the UK. Nor was it included in the Grouping arrangements of 1922, by which time Kynoch's had merged with Eley–Nobel Ltd, who then sold their business to Cory Bros Ltd, fuel and oil factors.

From 1939 wartime conditions again boosted the fortunes of the still independent Light Railway. The postwar years saw the Vacuum Oil Company take over the railway and close all save the Thames Haven to Coryton connection to what had become British Railways' network. This situation remained until the Mobil Oil Company took control in 1969, and it was they who closed down the railway through an Order dated 6 September 1971.

The Southminster Branch

The 16½-mile single-line branch ran from Wickford to Southminster. It was opened for goods on 1 June 1889 and to passengers on the following 1 July. The GER invested capital in the line, anticipating good returns since there was much potential, the management considered, for the area around Burnham-on-Crouch to become an important resort centred on yachting.

Many of the GER's expectations were realized as traffic flow increased and held up, even in the inter-war period when competition from road traffic was making life difficult for the LNER who had succeeded the GER by then. Much of the need for passenger-train involvement was from the fact that urban housing estates had been sited in the region, and this factor continued to influence the fortunes of the branch post-1945, so that the line became a well-used commuter line sharing in the revitalization programmes that followed after the end of steam traction for some Essex lines.

West Ham station, seen here on 17 March 1951 as a 4–4–2T No. 41936, built by the LMS in 1923, passes on a Down train with evidence of war–time damage to the station infrastructure still visible. *(H.C. Casserley)*

This scene shows Woodgrange Park station building, facing north on to the A118, Romford Road, mid-1950s. The railway here formed part of the first section of the LTSR, opened in 1854. Woodgrange Park was built 1893–94 in connection with the joint MR/LTSR Tottenham and Forest Gate Railway. The first trains called here on 9 July 1894. *(Lens of Sutton)*

Barking East Junction signal-box on the south side of the line is seen here, with the station out of sight to the right. The station was rebuilt between 1906 and 1908, during which time the crossing was replaced by an overbridge (February 1907); the box was abolished a year later. Signalling on the line between Barking and Upminster (opened 1885) was contracted to Easterbrook, Hanniford and Co., and included provision of the box in the picture. *(N. Bowdidge Collection)*

Barking station, LTSR, is seen here in spring 1908, looking east. The LTSR was quadrupled and electrified from Bromley to here between 1905 and 1908. In this view all the new works are nearly complete, including the yellow brick west box to the left. A LTSR rebuilt 37 class 4–4–2T waits to leave platform 3 for Fenchurch Street, while a GER class Y14 0–6–0 is exercising GER running powers over the line with a goods from Tilbury through platform 8. *(Lens of Sutton)*

These two views show Dagenham station, looking east, *c.* 1900. In the lower view an LTSR 51 class 4–4–2T is approaching on an Up train. The station opened on 1 May 1885 and became Dagenham East in 1932. LTSR section trains ceased to call here after electrification in June 1962 and the Up side buildings were demolished in 1982. *(Lens of Sutton)*

This view shows Dagenham Heathway District Line station looking west in LMS days. The LMS through lines are to the left; they opened the station for District Line trains only on 12 September 1932, primarily to serve the commuters on the local housing estate. The station became plain Heathway under the Eastern Region in 1949. *(Lens of Sutton)*

Upminster station is seen here from the Up platform, looking towards London. A Down slow train is approaching, and the stock for an Upminster–Romford train stands to the right. *(Lens of Sutton)*

Upminster, looking east from the main road bridge, *c.* 1911, with a scene of LTSR rebuilt 37 class 4–4–2T No. 40 *Benfleet* waits to leave the Romford branch platform with a stopping train to Barking. This loco was rebuilt in December 1910 (and renamed from *Black Horse Road*). Five members of the staff pose by the engine, while a sixth makes a blur on the photograph in the 6 ft way to the right. *(Lens of Sutton)*

This view shows Upminster Up side station buildings, with goods shed in the distance, *c.* 1900. The sod-cutting ceremony for the Barking–Upminster–Pitsea direct line was held by Upminster windmill on 11 October 1883. *(Lens of Sutton)*

East Horndon station, looking east, *c.* 1910. It was opened as a temporary terminus for the Upminster line on 1 May 1886, and was situated in what was then a remote area of Essex, being provided as a sop to Lord Petre who owned much land in the area. The buildings are the standard LTSR design for the line, compared with Laindon (below). The station underwent a name change to West Horndon at a later date. *(N. Bowdidge Collection)*

Laindon station is seen here at about noon on a summer's day, some time between 1907 and 1911. The Up Fenchurch Street station train is approaching behind a rebuilt 37 class 4–4–2T, unusually running bunker first on an Up train, *c.* 1900. Laindon was rebuilt as a three-platform station by the LMS in the mid-1930s. *(Lens of Sutton)*

This view shows Laindon station from the Up platform, looking towards London, *c.* 1900. As usual in these scenes, the station staff are called out *en masse* to pose for the cameraman *(Lens of Sutton)*

Pitsea Junction is seen here looking east towards Southend, *c.* 1935. The name Pitsea Junction only appeared on the station and was never used in timetables. The original route was opened on 1 July 1855. The curved platforms behind the staff are of the direct line to Upminster, opened on 1 June 1888. *(Lens of Sutton)*

The original LTSR station at Leigh-on-Sea was at the foot of a steep hill from the town centre and close to the beach. The site was severely restricted, and this view shows the goods yard and part of the beach as seen from the jetty. The goods vehicle farthest left is an LTSR fish van that has been converted from a cattle van, and is employed in shellfish carriage in the wicker baskets that can be seen by the railings where nets hang out to dry. This view dates from about 1910. *(N. Bowdidge Collection)*

This view shows the Down platform at Leigh-on-Sea looking towards Southend, between 1905 and 1910. When opened on 1 July 1855, the Up platform was opposite the Down, but the cramped conditions gave no room for expansion so it was necessary to build a new Up platform on the other side of the level-crossing in about 1903. This station was closed on 31 December 1933 and replaced by a new one half a mile to the west. *(Lens of Sutton)*

This scene of Southend-on-Sea station shows platforms 5 and 6 in 1899, with two 51 class 4–4–2Ts. No. 51 *Kentish Town* is on a Fenchurch Street via Tilbury train (in the foreground) while No. 59 *Holloway* is heading MR stock for St Pancras station in platform 6. The railway to Southend opened on 1 March 1856. *(Lens of Sutton)*

This longer view of Southend-on-Sea shows the Railway Hotel prominent in the background. The enlarged layout of 1899 can be clearly seen, including the 58-lever signal-box of that date. The rolling stock is mostly of MR design, possibly awaiting returning excursionists, and the date is considered to be in about 1908, rather than the year suggested by the postcard publisher. *(Lens of Sutton)*

Southend Pier, *c.* 1890. A horse-drawn car, which used a railway track system to carry passengers predated the electric railway, seen here, for which the Chelmsford-based manufacturers, Crompton Parkinson, supplied the rolling stock. *(Essex County Record Office)*

This scene shows the staff at Southend-on-Sea LT&SR station in 1882. The stationmaster of the day may be picked out, as he is wearing a silk hat and long overcoat. The train shed is behind the group, with a glazed *porte-cochère* shelter which had been recently added to the building. *(Essex County Record Office)*

Railway employees often created a social and sporting dimension to their work and a football team comprising LT&SR men from John Street, Southend is seen here in 1902. *(Essex County Record Office)*

This view of Thorpe Bay station shows the main forecourt, probably just after the opening on 1 July 1910. *(Lens of Sutton)*

Ex LTSR 4–4–2T No. 80 *Thundersley* in preservation condition, repainted in original livery, stands at Shoeburyness, having hauled a special train from Liverpool Street to commemorate the LT&S's centenary on 11 February 1956. *(D. Lawrence/H. Davies)*

The road approach to Shoeburyness station, 11 February 1956. A 2–6–4T stands behind the fence. *(D. Lawrence/H. Davies)*

Shoeburyness, the most easterly LTSR station, is shown here looking towards the buffer stops with a large gathering of staff, *c.* 1900. The War Office, among others, opposed plans to extend the railway to this point before the station opened on 1 February 1884. *(Lens of Sutton)*

LMSR Whitelegg 3P class 4–4–2T No. 2113 built subsequent to the grouping, in 1923, is seen here at Shoeburyness running shed on 27 June 1936. *(H.F. Wheeler/R. Carpenter)*

LTSR class 37 4–4–2T No. 43 *Great Ilford* on a train of fuel oil wagons from Thames Haven is shown heading towards London at Romford LTSR, *c.* 1903. The passenger platform is to the right, with the signal-box at its end. The first eight tank wagons belong to the GER and were built in 1897–8, and either carried 2,000 or 2,300 gallons of oil. *(HMRS/R. Hilton)*

Ockendon station, in LTSR days, is seen here looking south towards West Thurrock on the Tilbury line. The station was opened on 1 July 1892, having originally been authorized on 20 August 1883. *(Lens of Sutton)*

Tilbury station, shown here in about 1910, was rebuilt in 1906 and again later by the LMS. The large roof covered a spacious concourse and the covered way led down to the pier for the LTSR's Gravesend steamers. Steps and lifebelts are all marked with the company's initials. *(N. Bowdidge Collection)*

Tilbury shed (coded 33B in the Eastern Region of British Railways), is seen here on 11 February 1956. Ex-LTSR Whitelegg '69' class 3F 0–6–2T No. 41989 awaits its next duty. The whole of this fourteen-strong class were at ex-LT&SR sheds in 1955. *(D. Lawrence/H. Davies)*

Stephenson Locomotive Society Special at Thames Haven, headed by ex-LTSR 69 class 0–6–2T No. 41983 is seen here on 3 April 1954. Climbing into the loco is Inspector G. Hampshire of Plaistow, who joined the LTSR in June 1906 and retired in May 1954. The special was run to celebrate the centenary of the LTSR. The photographer, Philip J. Kelley, worked at Fenchurch Street Control office from 1949 to 1951. *(Philip J. Kelley)*

This shows the 10.50 a.m. Thames Haven to Ripple Lane oil train passing Thames Haven Junction on 20 March 1954, headed by ex-LNER Class J 17 No. 65566. *(Philip J. Kelley)*

In 1868 the Gas Light and Coke Company were permitted to build alongside the Thames in order to use seaborne coal to make coal gas and associated by-products works at Beckton. Neilson 0–4–0T No. 1, of 1892, was one of fourteen locomotives at the by-products disposal works. The livery was maroon with black and/or white lining. Seen here on 24 August 1957, No. 1 survived until 1968. *(R.M. Casserley)*

This scene shows the No. 2 Pier on 9 July 1927, with a group of enthusiasts riding towards the River Thames, hauled by a Neilson 0–4–0T. A 1-in-40 track connection with the ground-level system can be seen below the central semaphore signals, which had orange and blue spectacles to prevent any confusion with port and starboard colours by shipping on the Thames. *(H.C. Casserley)*

One of Beckton's 0–4–0 fireless locomotives No. 35, manufactured by Robert Stephenson Hawthorns in 1954, is shown here at Beckton on 24 August 1957. The high fire risk associated with the by-products such as phenols, creosote and tar, meant that fireless locomotives were used for duties involving these materials. An insulated pressure tank replaces the locomotive's boiler, for which high pressure steam was obtained from a stationary boiler at a safe distance away from operations. *(R.M. Casserley)*

The GLCC had large locomotive facilities at Beckton, including their own works, where No. 30, seen here on 9 July 1927, was constructed. The ex-ECR carriage, one of three used at Beckton, dates from 1860 and had a year previously been on royal duty when King George V and Queen Mary opened the new coal-handling plant in July 1926. *(H.C. Casserley)*

The Ford Motor Company of Dagenham maintained a fleet of wagons and locomotives. These two views show a 10-ton tank wagon of 1933 vintage (above) and a Peckett 0–4–0ST No. 1861 built at Bristol in 1934 stands on the lightweight running rails of Ford's internal system (below). *(Above: C. Roberts/HMRS; below: R.C. Riley)*

This view shows the wooden-planked platform at Kynochtown looking towards the explosives works, with a rear view of Kitson 0–4–0WT *Cordite* prior to the First World War. The low-roofed carriage is probably a rebuilt composite coach originally supplied by Kerr Stuart in 1901. *(Lens of Sutton)*

The Kitson 0–4–0WT *Cordite*, with the rebuilt composite coach, is seen here prior to the First World War. Built in 1893, the locomotive was purchased second-hand from the Barry Docks Co., South Wales. Water was carried in a well tank below the frames, as well as in two small side tanks. *(N. Bowdidge Collection)*

Kerr, Stuart 0–4–2T of the Corringham Light Railway poses for the camera on the marshes at Kynochtown in the early 1900s. *(N. Bowdidge Collection)*

The so-called 'Kynochtown Mail' train on the Corringham Light Railway, enters Kynochtown station in the early 1900s, hauled by Kerr, Stuart 0–4–2T 'Kyanite' with the 'toastrack' carriage bringing up the rear. *(N. Bowdidge Collection)*

The workhorse of the Essex freight services, Holden class J17 0–6–0 No. 65555, of Stratford shed, runs into Shenfield from Southend Victoria on 9 July 1955. Note the overhead wires to the left, along with colour light signalling. *(Philip J. Kelley)*

Billericay in the first decade of the twentieth century with a GER T19 class 2–4–0 fitted with an oil-fuel tender. The view is from the Stock Road overbridge at the country end of the station. Billericay was opened for goods on 19 November 1888 and for passengers on 1 January 1889. The goods shed is in the distance beyond the passenger overbridge, which is unusual for the GER in being a completely enclosed structure. Goods traffic ceased on 5 June 1967. *(N. Bowdidge Collection)*

The station staff at Wickford, *c.* 1910, face the photographer who is standing on the Wick Lane level-crossing at the Southend side of the station. Wickford was a terminus for passenger trains until 1 July 1889, when the Southminster line was opened for passenger traffic, the line to Southend following this event on 1 October 1889. *(Lens of Sutton)*

This view shows the road frontage at Rayleigh station, looking from the road out of the town centre, *c.* 1900. The road swings to the right behind the horse-drawn vehicle, passes under the railway and then leads to Wickford. *(N. Bowdidge Collection)*

Rayleigh station in GER days, looking towards Wickford, shows typical architectural features in the main station buildings – as can be seen in other places on the 'New Essex' route to Southend. *(Lens of Sutton)*

A raft of wagons have become derailed at a catch point near Rayleigh, *c.* 1900. The signal for the catch point is to the left of the furthest member of the permanent way staff. *(HMRS/R. Hilton)*

A Southend-bound train is in Hockley station with a GER 2–4–0 at its head. A porter and a postman pose for the photographer on the platform. Hockley opened with the Wickford to Southend section on 1 October 1889 as part of the 'New Essex' promotions of 1883, designed in this case to regain access to Southend after the GER ceased working the LTSR line to Southend in 1880. Hockley closed to goods on 5 June 1967, while the signal-box on the left was reduced to a ground frame in 1937. *(Lens of Sutton)*

This view, looking towards Rochford, *c.* 1911, is from the station signal-box at Prittlewell. The bridge in the distance was replaced in the late 1920s by what is now known as Eastern Avenue. *(HMRS/R. Hilton)*

GER class D56 4–4–0 No. 1790 hurries the 2.00 p.m. Liverpool Street to Southend away from Prittlewell on 17 April 1911, when the locomotive was only two months old. The burnished smokebox door reinforcing ring would show up well on the royal blue livery with red lining and polished brasswork. *(LCGB/K. Nunn)*

Class B17/6 4–6–0 No. 61612 *Houghton Hall* on the 3.07 p.m. Shenfield to Southend (Victoria) leaves Prittlewell station on 2 July 1955. The ex-GER code, using one violet and one white disc on the buffer beam to denote a local Shenfield to Southend train, is still in use. *(Philip J. Kelley)*

This view shows Prittlewell, looking towards the station. Gresley ex-LNER class B17/1 No. 61608 *Gunton* leaves Prittlewell towards Southend with the 1.53 p.m. ex-Liverpool Street, on 2 July 1955. *(LCGB/K. Nunn)*

Class K3/3 2–6–0 No. 61880 leaves Southend (Victoria) on 2 July 1955 passing the loco shed seen above the train's carriages. The K3 class is an ex-GNR design and as such only worked the Essex LNER lines on a regular basis from 1938. *(Philip J. Kelley)*

The station forecourt at Southend Victoria, *c.* 1910. The design was by Ashbee and similar in style to Norwich Thorpe, Hertford and Felixstowe, particularly the combination of brick and stonework. *(Lens of Sutton)*

Small passenger locomotives of both the Eastern and Midland Regions of BR line up at Southend (ex-GER) shed on 2 July 1955, with class N7/3 0–6–2T No. 69701 and class 3P 4–4–2T No. 41952. The N7 was one of its class rebuilt in 1943 from a similar N7/2 group. *(Philip J. Kelley)*

Southend (Victoria), with 4–6–0 Class 'B12/3' No. 61546 waiting to depart in the London direction. This locomotive was rebuilt with a round-topped boiler, to Sir Nigel Gresley's design, in 1932. Its origin was in S.D. Holden's GER small Belpaire design that was introduced in 1911. *(Lens of Sutton)*

CHAPTER FIVE

THE MID-ESSEX BRANCH LINES

This view of Haverhill (South) station was probably from a photographic survey of the CV&HR line in the winter of 1882/3. The original intention was to link the line with that of the LNWR at Cambridge, so Haverhill was not originally intended to become a terminus The platform was little used by passengers, as the link with the GER via the spur to Haverhill (North) was opened in 1865 and most CV&HR passenger trains terminated there in the GER station.
To the left of one of two examples of very rudimentary stop blocks is a grounded body of an outside framed vehicle, suggested to be the remains of the line's original brake-van and in use as a PW hut. Out of picture to the left was the locomotive 'works'. The station building is believed to have been erected as a temporary measure to facilitate opening the station. The goods shed to the right dominates the whole scene.
(Lens of Sutton/A. Corder-Birch)

The Bishop's Stortford, Dunmow and Braintree Line

The route between Bishop's Stortford and Dunmow was opened by the GER on 22 February 1869. The original company had fallen into financial difficulties and wasrescued by absorption into the GER in 1865. The first scheme contained a branch from Dunmow to Epping, and later an interchange at Dunmow with the proposed Central Essex Light Railway (planned between 1901 and 1908) was considered but not implemented. A Halt was added at Hockerill, near Bishop's Stortford, in 1910, and in 1922 Halts were opened at Stane Street (between Hockerhill and Takeley) and Bannister Green (between Felstead and Rayne). Easton Lodge station was a special provision to be convenient for the Earl and Countess of Warwick at their nearby mansion. Locos of the 2–4–2T type predominated on the route. LNER Class F3 ('Jubilee' tank) No. 1067 was at Braintree shed in 1922 and the GER Class Y65 (LNER Class F7) were another type used for a time.

Passenger services in this underpopulated area were never going to bring a great revenue, in spite of a usual five a day, latterly seven passenger trains per day, along the 18-mile line. Felstead was the major source of goods traffic on the branch with a large sugar-beet factory for which a fifty-wagon passing loop and shunting spur was provided by the LNER in 1926. The regular passenger service ceased to run after Saturday 1 March 1952, although excursion trains to Clacton and Southend continued to use the branch, while Braintree developed eventually as the terminus for the Witham electrified service. In July 1960 the prototype 'Road Railer' combination vehicle was tested by British Railways on the branch. Goods services were withdrawn in piecemeal fashion, from Rayne (8 December 1964), Felstead to Takeley (18 April 1966), Easton Lodge to Dunmow (1 April 1969), Braintree to Felstead (20 June 1970) and, finally, Bishop's Stortford to Easton Lodge (February 1972).

Two Branches from Witham

A railway from Maldon to Braintree via Witham was proposed in 1845 and authorized in the next year. This plan included a crossing on the flat of the Eastern Counties Railway route east of Witham. The Maldon Company could not find the financial backing to complete construction and so the ECR stepped in to finish both the line to Maldon and also the northern section to Braintree, both opened in 1848, although through traffic between Braintree and Maldon involved a reversal of trains at Witham.

In 1889 further railway developments took place in connection with the 'New Essex Lines'. These included the construction of avoiding curves at both Witham and Maldon, in order to make through running from Colchester to the lines south of Witham. The intended traffic did not develop, however, nor did Maldon blossom as a port or a holiday resort. The Colchester to Southend services via the avoiding lines only lasted until 1895, when the curves became redundant and were closed.

A service of eight passenger trains each way on weekdays was maintained by the LNER through the inter-war years. This level of operation was increased after 1945 and reached a peak of seventeen each way on the introduction of the DMUs in 1959, but were withdrawn altogether in 1964 when the intermediate stations were closed completely. Freight services from Maldon lingered, with some activity until 18 April 1966. The branch to Braintree from Witham, although scheduled for closure under Dr Beeching's rationalization programme, has seen unprecedented growth and modernization. In 1869 the line was diverted so that through running to Bishop's Stortford could take place via a new Braintree station, the old one becoming the goods yard.

The Sudbury and Haverhill Line

The Colchester, Stour Valley, Sudbury and Halstead Company was incorporated in 1846 to construct a 12-mile line from the ECR station at Marks Tey to Sudbury, with intermediate stations at Bures and Chappel. The Company was also empowered to construct a 5¾-mile branch from Chappel to Halstead, but its powers later lapsed as expenditure on construction, particularly in building Chappel Viaduct, prevented a start on the Halstead link and a west-facing junction at Marks Tey. The Sudbury route was formally opened on 2 July 1849, on lease to the Eastern Union Railway and then, on 1 January 1854, the Eastern Counties Railway took over all the lines of the EUR, including the Stour Valley line. The next development was for the line to be absorbed by the GER on 1 July 1898.

In the early '50s the line was worked by a steady stream of ex-GER locomotives on the passenger trains, including 'Claud Hamilton' 4–4–0s, 'Intermediate' 2–4–0s, Holden 2–4–2Ts and J15 0–6–0s, which also provided motive power for the pick-up goods service that still existed at that time. A few through goods used the line between Whitemoor Yards and Colchester, and on these the larger Holden 0–6–0s and 'WD' 2–8–0s were noted. Excursion trains too, for example from Cambridge to Clacton, hauled by a 4–6–0, such as a 'Sandringham', were part of the summer scene at this period.

In the early 1960s loss of the Colne Valley line traffic, as well as the Bury St Edmunds to Long Melford closure, meant that only Colchester to Cambridge trains remained. Some stations on the line became unstaffed halts, while conductor guards on DMUs aimed at economy measures in the 1960s. Freight services south of Sudbury virtually disappeared by the late winter of 1964. After some prevarication, Sudbury's remaining link with the Cambridge district, via Shelford, closed completely on 6 March 1967, leaving the Sudbury to Marks Tey stub to survive against all the apparent odds.

The Colne Valley and Halstead Light Railway

The first section of the CV&HR to be opened was between Chappel and Wakes Colne, on the GER's Marks Tey to Sudbury line, and Halstead. This was in April 1860, but prior to this authority had been added to the CV&HR Act of 1856 to extend beyond Halstead to Haverhill. The additional route was then opened in stages, starting with the line to Hedingham (July 1861) then to Yeldham (May 1862) and, finally, to Haverhill (May 1863). Between 1865 and 1866 none other than Sir Daniel Gooch was in charge of operations under a contract. At the same time the GER had made their own plans to link their Cambridge to London main line to their own station at Haverhill, about half a mile away from the CV&HR's across the border in Suffolk.

In spite of a connecting spur line linking the two stations at Haverhill, authorized in 1863, there were attempts by the CV&HR to stymie the GER's plans for a rival line to Colchester via Sudbury. However, driven by failing finances which led to bankruptcy, the CV&HR became far more agreeable towards the GER and shared various facilities including maintenance of rolling stock at Stratford works. The line became absorbed into the LNER in 1923, and Haverhill (CV&HR) station was closed in 1924 as were Halstead works and depot, along with some pruning of the rolling stock. Geographically, the line appeared well placed to serve as a through route from the Midlands to the Essex coast, but weak bridges restricted this possibility.

The CV&HR was one of several Essex lines to see an upsurge of traffic under wartime conditions when several USAF bases were sited within a short distance of the railway. After the Second World War passenger traffic declined, and the introduction of DMUs in 1959 did nothing to woo back customers. Consequently passenger trains were withdrawn on 1 January 1962, the section between Yeldham and Haverhill closing completely. Freight services struggled on over the remnant of the line, but on 28 December 1964 they ceased between Halstead and Yeldham, followed by complete closure on 19 April 1965.

The Kelvedon and Tiptree Branch

The Kelvedon, Tiptree and Tollesbury Pier Light Railway, a 10-mile long line, was one of the direct results of the Light Railways Act of 1896 which sought to encourage the development of railway transport in rural areas by reducing the capital costs of construction. This was achieved through having simpler and fewer requirements to satisfy the Railway Inspectorate and thereby needing a smaller financial outlay on railway infrastructure. Supporters pointed to the anticipated traffic from the fruit-growing around the Tiptree district, where the Wilkins' jam factory was situated, and in addition the possible development of Tollesbury Pier as a yachting centre on the River Blackwater.

The K&TLR was authorized under a Light Railway Act dated 29 January 1901 and construction started in 1903, with the first section from Kelvedon to Tollesbury village opened in October 1904 and worked by the GER. However, the 1½-mile extension over the marshy banks of the Blackwater estuary to the Pier was not ready at the time of opening.

One method of saving money on a light railway was to allow unmanned road crossings and this was true of the K&T, where the train crew had the duty of operating the gates where these were provided. Another saving was made by using obsolete coach bodies for both goods and passenger shelters at stations along the route. Signals were provided only at Kelvedon.

After the development of local bus services from the early 1920s a decline in fortunes for the K&T began. The Tollesbury Pier section only lasted until 1921 and, although freight traffic was reasonably abundant in certain seasons, the mixed train service with a (nominal) speed restriction of 16 mph could not compete. The Second World War elevated the pier section to play a role in the coastal defence system, with the presence of four War Department locomotives complete with mobile guns. Passenger services ceased on 7 May 1951 and goods services were withdrawn beyond Tudwick Road fruit-collection sidings. The line was finally closed on 1 October 1962.

Takeley station looking towards Bishop's Stortford on 31 July 1960 with the ex-GER lower quadrant signal in the 'off' position. The station building of 1891 is of the '1865' style with distictive decorative brickwork consisting of slightly projecting quoins, string courses and window dressings. Ornate stonework around the windows was another feature of the station architecture. *(Philip J. Kelley)*

Easton Lodge, *c.* 1920. This was a station specially built for the family and guests of the Earl and Countess of Warwick. It was associated with the movements of Edwardian high society, in particular HRH Prince of Wales. *(Lens of Sutton)*

Dunmow station retains many ex-GER features including the water column near the camera and the stylish water tower beyond the main station building, April 1957. The last passenger train to leave Dunmow was the 8.15 p.m. from Bishop's Stortford on 1 March 1952, consisting of two ex-GER vestibuled carriages headed by F5 class No. 67211 and accompanied by passengers in fancy dress and exploding detonators. *(Philip J. Kelley)*

Dunmow station from the roadbridge, *c.* 1910. Opened on 22 February 1869, the goods facilities include three loading gauges on either side of the running line. Goods traffic was retained until 1 April 1969, long after passenger closure. The starting signal has spectacle glasses and lamp separated from the signal arm. *(Lens of Sutton)*

Rayne station looking east, with a short goods approaching and the goods shed and yard in the far background, *c.* 1910. The station buildings are fine examples of the GER's '1865' style of architecture with, in the case of this line, stone lintels on stone verticals surrounding the windows, those downstairs displaying a keystone feature. *(Lens of Sutton)*

Ex-LNER Worsdell class F5 2–4–2T No. 67188 waits at Braintree station facing west, *c.* 1953. The F5 class were rebuilt versions of class F4 2–4–2T with a higher boiler pressure. *(Lens of Sutton)*

Cressing station (known as Bulford until 1911), looking towards Bishop's Stortford in BR days. A concrete signal post supports an arm that protects the level crossing. *(Lens of Sutton)*

White Notley station situated between Witham and Cressing. It was opened on 2 November 1848 and in the photograph the building to the right of the signal-box is the original station building. The signal-box dates from the early 1890s, and with no goods sidings to control it was only needed to run the level-crossing and station signals. Gardening must have been a major preoccupation at this station. *(Lens of Sutton)*

Two views of Wickham Bishops looking towards Witham from the Witham–Maldon road overbridge, *c.* 1910. The station opened under the name of Wickham along with the whole route in 1848. The signal-box was taken out of use in 1940 when the signalling was rationalized and until that date the signalman-porter occupied a distinctive station house (top left). A small waiting room and toilet were provided within for the travelling public. Shunting goods into the loop siding on the left involved some complicated manoeuvres for the train crew. Inward goods consisted mainly of wheat and seed potatoes for Matthews Mill, brewer's grains for D.B. Smith, Wickham Hall and road surfacing grit for ECC. Outward traffic was mainly sugar-beet and, at times, peas. *(Lens of Sutton)*

Langford Station.
The only Station in England having a Station Mistress.

Langford station with its claim to uniqueness advertised, *c.* 1910. The station was referred to in an accident report of 1869 as a 'Flag station' when GER loco No. 152 derailed soon after passing on the last train from the Colchester show, carrying 70–80 passengers. The single fatality was the fireman while the driver was badly injured. *(Lens of Sutton)*

Langford and Ulting station looking towards Witham, *c.* 1957. Renamed Langford and Ulting on 1 July 1923, it eventually became an unmanned halt. *(Lens of Sutton)*

Waggon and Maschinenbau 4-wheel Railbus leaves Maldon East on 6 April 1957, passing the goods shed on its way to Witham. These German railbuses were introduced in an ultimately unsuccessful attempt by British Railways to revive the flagging economy of the passenger service on the Maldon East to Witham line. *(D. Lawrence via H. Davies)*

Maldon West station entrance, *c.* 1910. The branch from Woodham Ferrers to Maldon West was opened on 1 October 1889. Maldon West closed during the First World War as an economy measure from May 1916 to 1 August 1919. Closure to passenger traffic happened again on 10 September 1939 although freight services remained until 1959. *(Lens of Sutton)*

The road approach to Cold Norton station, looking towards Woodham Ferrers, *c.* 1910. There are similarities in the architecture between this station and Battlesbridge. The goods store has the more usual hipped roof design. In the distance the goods yard entrance is visible as are three loading gauges. The end loading bay contains two carriage trucks. *(Lens of Sutton)*

Cold Norton station for Purleigh and Stow Maries looking south, *c.* 1910. It opened for all traffic on 1 October 1899, closed to passengers on 10 September 1939 and to freight on 1 April 1953. *(Lens of Sutton)*

Fambridge station in GER days, looking towards Southminster, *c.* 1912. Opened to goods traffic on 1 June 1889 and to passengers a month later, it closed to goods traffic on 4 October 1965 and most of the station buildings were demolished in 1968. When the line was electrified and resignalled in 1986 the signal-box was removed. The footbridge was the standard design for the line. *(Lens of Sutton)*

The station buildings at Battlesbridge (opened under the name of Rettendon) from the approach road, *c.* 1910. The style is typical of smaller stations on the Southend, Southminster and Maldon West lines. At the right-hand end of the station building is the office known as 'the brake goods store'. *(Lens of Sutton)*

Battlesbridge station from the track looking towards Woodham Ferrers, *c.* 1910. There is a good view of the goods shed and the weighbridge hut in the distance, and it is interesting to see how the telegraph wires unusually use a signal post to act as a support past the station building. *(Lens of Sutton)*

Ex-LNER class C12 4–4–2T No. 67385, an Ivatt GNR-designed locomotive, leaves Marks Tey station with the 11.52 a.m. train to Cambridge via Sudbury on 30 October 1954. *(Philip J. Kelley)*

At Chappel and Wakes Colne, change for the Colne Valley Railway is announced on the station running-in board to the left. Ex-LNER class J15 0–6–0 No. 65448 waits to depart with a Cambridge to Colchester train on 26 May 1956. Spacious goods accommodation is seen to the right of the overbridge, where traffic was particularly heavy at times of the sugar-beet season in winter and the fruit and vegetable season in summer. *(H.C. Casserley)*

The Sudbury line was built as a double-track line in readiness for further promotions and included the highly costly Chappel Viaduct, the largest in Essex, which was opened for passenger traffic on 2 July 1849. Each of thirty arches has a span of 35 ft, 7 million bricks were reputedly used, and the cost was £32,000. *(Philip J. Kelley)*

Bures station between Chappel and Wakes Colne and Sudbury looking towards Sudbury in BR days, *c.* 1955. Although a token station (the porter in the lower photograph, to the right of the knot of waiting passengers, has the token over his shoulder), Bures has only one platform and cannot be used as a crossing-station for passenger trains. The station building is an original Colchester, Stour Valley, Sudbury and Halstead Railway structure, and the belfry which once housed the train arrival bell can be seen above the roof of the shed. Traffic of all description had ceased by the end of December 1964. *(Lens of Sutton)*

This view of Colne Valley Junction, Haverhill, is dated *c.* 1918. The GER Stour Valley line leads off to the left, while the GER link to the Colne Valley railway bears right. Hamlet Road viaduct is in the background and an unidentified CVR 2–4–2T passes the signal-box. *(HMRS/R. Hilton)*

Great Yeldham station on the extension of the route between Halstead and Haverhill (South), is shown here in about 1875 looking towards Birdbrook and very much in original condition, without a signal-box but with the important addition of a water supply on the platform served by a wind pump and water tower. The stationmaster in view is probably John Willoughby Lee, later stationmaster at Halstead. *(A. Corder-Birch Collection)*

This view shows Great Yeldham station in 1919, looking towards Castle Hedingham. In the extreme background is the brick bridge at Lark Hill Farm. Stationmaster Joseph Pittock is in the foreground, in uniform, second from the left. Edward Steward is the signalman outside his box, while the porter pulling a trolley is Basil (George) Argent. Third from the left is a Mr Martin, a milkman from Stambourne. *(A. Corder-Birch Collection)*

Hedingham Brick and Tile and Terra Cotta works siding, *c.* 1894. Hedingham 'reds' were well known and used extensively at home and abroad. The man on top of the kiln is John Corder and on the left is his son, Edward. Daniel Cornish, manager for proprietor Mark Gentry, is in the foreground wearing a bowler hat. Mark Gentry was one of a number of proposers for the Central Essex Light Railway in the 1890s. *(A. Corder-Birch Collection)*

This view shows the sidings adjacent to the joinery works of Messrs Rippers before the First World War. Rippers commenced business in Castle Hedingham towards the end of the nineteenth century and moved to the site shown in about 1900. Rippers were taken over by Bowaters in the 1970s and became Bowater Rippers Ltd. *(A. Corder-Birch Collection)*

The Colne Valley Railway train is seen here between Sible Hedingham and Halstead, *c.* 1895. The site is the Hedingham side of the road bridge which went over the railway. The locomotive is an 0–4–2T, CV&HR No. 1 with supplementary side tanks. *(A. Corder-Birch Collection)*

This scene of Halstead station in the early 1930s shows the quite extensive goods sidings of this, the principal intermediate station on the CV&HR. The layout was extended and remodelled from the original over a period of time, but still incorporated the original station building of 1862 designed by Joseph Cubitt and incorporating red, white and blue brickwork. *(A. Corder-Birch Collection)*

Earls Colne station is shown here in 1906, with a CV&HR tank loco in the station. The new brick station buildings, which were erected in 1903, stand up behind the original wooden shed. *(Lens of Sutton)*

This excursion party is about to set off from Earls Colne station, *c*. 1905, not long after the station was rebuilt in 1903 and renamed Colne instead of Ford Gate. In 1905 its name changed again to Earls Colne. Passengers had a Mr Hunt to thank for their improved facilities, as he donated land and assisted greatly with the finances that enabled the building work to take place. *(A.Corder-Birch Collection)*

Kelvedon low level, *c.* 1948, facing south-west and looking up the goods-only gradient connection to the main line station. The passenger facilities consist of a waiting shed, toilet and a low platform. A corrugated-iron engine shed with coal stage and water tower (centre picture) were provided to service the branch locomotive. A small signal cabin stands on the left. *(Lens of Sutton)*

The GER cartage staff at Kelvedon goods shed, *c.* 1907. Duties included a delivery service of small parcels around the district which arrived on both branch and main line services. Horse traction was in its heyday for Essex railway goods depots at this period. *(N. Bowdidge Collection)*

LNER J65 class 0–6–0T No. 7247 awaits departure from Kelvedon low level station on a mixed train to Tollesbury, *c.* 1938. When the branch opened a GER 0–4–2T, No. 25, was used but was soon replaced by J67 class 0–6–0Ts which ran converted to 2–4–0Ts by the removal of the front coupling rod. The purpose of this was to save wear on the wheels when travelling around the sharp curves which abounded along the branch. *(Lens of Sutton)*

LNER class J68 0–6–0T No. 7045 is seen at Kelvedon low level station, 1930s. The train includes the coaches which had been transferred from the Wisbech and Upwell Tramway line in 1928. These vehicles featured end platforms with ornate iron railings around them for passenger safety. The seating plan inside the carriages was similar to a tramcar, while a guard issued tickets on the train as it travelled. *(Lens of Sutton)*

GER class R24 No. 391 running as a 2–4–0T heads towards Tollesbury with the 12.30 p.m. from Kelvedon, near Feering, on 31 March 1910. The distant signal (fixed) for the Kelvedon home signal is in view. The gates across the main London to Colchester road were operated by the train crews. (LCGB/K. Nunn)

Looking east from the site of Feering Halt. Beyond the visitor the line drops away at 1-in-50, the ruling gradient, towards Tiptree. At one time the platform was provided with an old bus body for accommodation. Just beyond the halt, a siding formerly went off in a trailing direction from Kelvedon. (*Hugh Davies)*

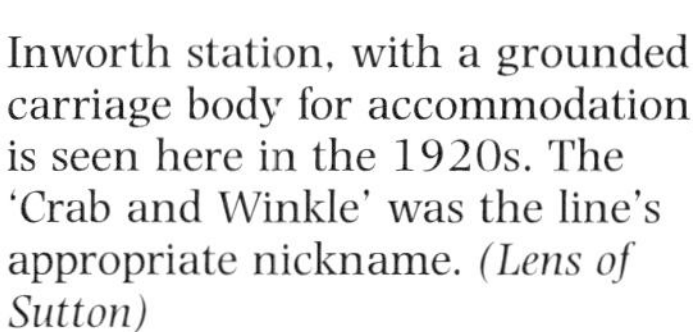

Inworth station, with a grounded carriage body for accommodation, is seen here in the 1920s. The 'Crab and Winkle' was the line's appropriate nickname. *(Lens of Sutton)*

Tiptree station is shown here looking towards Tollesbury, *c.* 1901. Tiptree was the principal intermediate station along the branch, with a goods yard connected into Messrs Wilkins' jam factory. Many of the components of a light railway can be detected, with a mixed train approaching a low platform with basic, wooden buildings. The rails used were of lighter weight than on a main line permanent way. *(Lens of Sutton)*

Tiptree station looking towards Tollesbury in June 1948. Ex-LNER class J69/1 No. 8636 awaits departure for Kelvedon while some of the railway staff take their ease on the platform seat. A young lady stands by the diminutive ex-Wisbech and Upwell Tramway coach.*(Lens of Sutton)*

CHAPTER SIX

BETWEEN THE RIVERS STOUR & COLNE

The train ferry berth at Harwich was relocated from Richborough, Kent, where it had served as a strategic supply point during the First World War. Of the three original ex–WD ferries bought by the GER, only one survived the Second World War. The ferry service was introduced in 1924 for freight only as a result of a partnership between the GER and Belgian State Railways.
In this view one of the replacement vessels, BR (Eastern Region) train ferry, MV Essex*, is moored alongside a wooden jetty looking out to the River Stour at Harwich harbour, working on the Harwich–Zeebrugge service, on 9 July 1955. To allow for the difference in tides an adjustable bridge was provided as part of the berthing facilities, allowing rail access on deck at most times. Vans of perishable products tended to be the main cargo, but in this case the tank wagons containing inflammable liquids were positioned at the open end of the deck for safety reasons.* (Philip J. Kelley)

Tendring Hundred Railway

The Tendring Hundred Railway Company was incorporated in 1859. Its primary development was a 2½-mile route to Wivenhoe, originating from the harbour branch line to the Hythe. From 1863 the GER operated the line for 70 per cent of the receipts. The next development occurred on 1 March 1866, when the Tendring Hundred Railway completed a short spur to St Botolph's station in Colchester from junctions at the Hythe and East Gate. The growth of Walton as a seaside resort was quickly accelerated in 1843 when the Eastern Counties Railway reached Colchester, greatly assisted by the multi-faceted commercial enterprise shown by Peter Schuler Bruff. Bruff had already established his railway engineering credentials by masterminding the construction of Chappel Viaduct and Ipswich Tunnel, and followed these achievements by becoming the entrepreneur who expanded the attractions and facilities of Walton.

In 1863 authorization for the Tendring Hundred Railway to extend to Walton was granted by Parliament. Unfortunately for the THR, the plans already agreed for the route of the Wivenhoe and Brightlingsea Railway blocked their entry into Wivenhoe. However, by 1864 the Wivenhoe and Brightlinsea promoters had defaulted on their construction agreement allowing the THR to step into the breach and forge an entry into Wivenhoe from the Walton direction. Time-consuming litigation then followed between the THR and the W&BR which, with the bankruptcy of their contractor, Munro, delayed completion of the single line to Walton until 1867. By this date P.S. Bruff had taken over as the THR's engineer as part of his determined effort to realize his aspirations and have the railway to play a significant role in the commercial development of Walton. The line was an immediate success. Cheap fare excursion trains for the 2-hour journey to Walton from London became very popular in the mid-1870s, 'Encouraging the seaside habit' as the GER posters of the day enthused.

The THR was absorbed by the GER on 1 July 1883, a year after the independent Clacton-on-Sea Railway opened its 4½-mile line to a junction with the Walton line at Thorpe-le-Soken. At this stage, in 1888, Frinton gained its own station.

During the 1890s the 'day-tripper' trade continued to expand, with a bonus for the GER accruing from the establishment of commuting to work in London from seaside in Essex as a possible way of life. Two daily through trains to Liverpool Street station were timetabled at this period to cater for these commuters from the Walton district. This rapidly increasing passenger traffic brought the need to double the track or else to provide passing loops. A Saturday midnight 'supper' train express to Clacton started a trend for restaurant-car services along the line, which culminated in summer 1922 with a full Sunday Pullman service, the 'Clacton Pullman'. The LNER, after the grouping, rebuilt Clacton station and completed colour-light signals between Thorpe-le-Soken and Clacton by 1941 as their major contribution to the route's infrastructure.

British Railways' first major innovation was the introduction of a 'Clacton Interval Service', run hourly in the summer from 1950. The LNER had seen fit to leave the motive power for the line largely in the hands of the old GER designs but BR, with their 'Britannia' Pacific class along with modern B1 4–6–0s, enabled further accelerations of train times in the 1950s. By the late 1950s the Tendring Hundred line had been chosen as the testbed for a different system of overhead electric traction supply, and the way forward was open for through train electric services to London.

The Brightlingsea Branch

The Wivenhoe and Brightlingsea branch was the poor neighbour of the other two well-patronized routes to the North Sea coast in the region between the Stour and the Colne. After a period of uncomfortable relations with the GER, the W&BR was bought up by the GER in June 1893. The harbour at Brightlingsea could not be developed in the manner anticipated, largely owing to the lack of deep water. However, the oyster traffic along with fish consignments and a certain amount of passenger excursion use kept the line in business into the 1950s, despite a catastrophic amount of damage to the infrastructure in the great flood of January 1953. BR made efforts to improve the passenger service via Colchester by the introduction of diesel powered units, but road competition proved too great and the line closed totally on 15 June 1964.

The Harwich Branch

A railway connection to the port of Harwich was high on the agenda for many entrepreneurs of the region. The Eastern Counties Railway had plans for a direct route from Colchester in 1836. Another scheme, with a junction at Ardleigh, was approved at first by Parliament only to be rejected by the House of Lords.

The Eastern Union Railway had their rival scheme from Manningtree approved in 1847 subject to an arrangement for leasing to the ECR. However, the ECR then took over the EUR in January 1854, prior to the opening of Harwich branch in August of that year. Although a terminus at Harwich appeared to be a great prize, costs of construction soared above expectations and receipts did not achieve high enough levels – even with the ECR's entry into both coastal and cross channel shipping trades. The takeover of the ECR by the GER in 1862 finally gave impetus to the development of the Harwich sea terminal. Success followed to such an extent that the railway layout at Harwich became no longer able to provide for the volume of traffic and so, on reclaimed land 1½ miles up the River Stour, the port of Parkeston was established.

By the time of Parkeston Quay's opening in 1883, a deviation in the line was in place to enable a rail connection to be made and the whole branch had been doubled. At the same time, a spur to allow trains on to the branch at Manningtree from the Ipswich direction paved the way for the running of cross-country trains, such as the unofficially named 'North Country Continental'. After playing a vital strategic role in the First and Second World Wars, traffic along the line reached a high point, featuring luxurious and sharply timed boat trains, latterly to a new terminal at Parkeston West (opened on 1 October 1934). In addition, a ground-breaking inter-continental train ferry service from Harwich was introduced in 1924. After the war Harwich became the port of entry for the British Army on the Rhine (BAOR) and a muted return to the numerous pre-war boat trains came about, including a freshly named 'Day Continental'.

From January 1968 the line between Harwich Town and Parkestone East was worked as a single track. Any worries about the immediate future at a time of much shrinkage of the rail system were removed in the mid-1980s by the electrification scheme, and the development of a substantial traffic initiated by the Freightliner service.

Gresley class B17/2 No. 2822 *Alnwick Castle* built in January 1931 takes the Harwich line at Manningtree on 'The Flushing Continental', including Pullman cars, *c.* 1931. It was second in importance as a boat train after the 'Hook Continental'. *(LCGB/K. Nunn)*

Bradfield station looking towards Manningtree, *c.* 1910. The station did not appear in public timetables until two years after the line had opened. The signal-box contained twelve levers and closed in 1950, while the station, which had no goods facilities, closed on 2 July 1956. *(Lens of Sutton)*

Parkeston Quay station looking towards Harwich, *c.* 1910. The station was named after C.H. Parkes, chairman of the GER since 1875, and was opened on 15 March 1883. To reach the purpose-built site for the continental boat services on the Isle of Ray, the original direct line to Harwich had been diverted 3 miles east of Wrabness station. The GER hotel in the centre of the view eventually closed in 1965. *(Lens of Sutton)*

A second view of Parkeston Quay station, looking towards Manningtree and showing carriages in the small Down side bay platform, *c.* 1910. Parkeston was built as a replacement for Harwich when rail-borne traffic became too great for the latter port to handle, and a railway town grew up. Various enlargements of the site have been carried out until a complete refurbishment took place in the 1960s. *(Lens of Sutton)*

B1 class 4–6–0 No. 61233 of Stratford shed (30A) rolls the Down 'Day Continental' into Parkeston Quay on 9 July 1955. This train, the post-war successor to the 'Flushing Continental' boat train, left Liverpool Street at 10.45 a.m. and covered the journey in 75 minutes. The headboard displays the Dutch flag alongside the Union Jack. *(Philip J. Kelley)*

B1 class 4–6–0 No. 61233 is seen here on the second phase of its day's work, on 9 July 1955, after working the Down 'Day Continental'. It returned to London with the Up 'Scandinavian' at 1.30 p.m., in connection with sailings from Esjberg. Before 1930 this train was called the 'Esjberg Continental'. *(Philip J. Kelley)*

In this scene of Parkeston four-road engine shed, looking towards the station (left) and the quay warehouses, GER Class Y14 0–6–0s are on shed in some number, along with smaller tank locomotives, *c.* 1911. Among the coal wagons to the right and towards the end of the siding is a clerestory-roofed van designed especially for the transport of butter. *(HMRS/R. Hilton)*

Two rail-mounted steam cranes are in use to lower a new turntable into position at Parkeston, on 1 December 1912. Bowler-hatted inspectors are there to supervise the procedures. *(HMRS/R. Hilton)*

This view of Parkeston Quay before 1907 shows several of the GER's cross-channel fleet, including the *Colchester* built in 1888 that was used on the Antwerp service. Seized by the German navy while on Rotterdam to Tilbury duty, the *Colchester* was then torpedoed by the Royal Navy while flying the German flag, finally to be salvaged and used in the Baltic for mine-laying. The close connection of the quay with the railway can be seen on the right. *(N. Bowdidge Collection)*

This scene shows Dovercourt Bay station, looking west from the footbridge, *c.* 1905. The Victoria Hotel is to the left, and carts are being loaded in the goods siding. Typical GER design buffer stops terminate the right-hand siding. The station signal-box stands at the far end of the Down platform and behind is the tall cement-works chimney which the GER helped to develop as an industry. *(HMRS/R. Hilton)*

Dovercourt Bay station is seen here in BR(E) days, with a closer view of the station signal-box looking towards Harwich. A colour-light signal under the canopy shares control with the semaphore on the Down platform. *(Lens of Sutton)*

The GER maintained a number of hotels and the one on the left of this view at Harwich shows the building in about 1950, many years after closure as a railway hotel in 1923. Harwich was the first of the GER hotels to open (1865), but was never very profitable for them. It served as a naval hospital in the First World War when it was of great value to wounded sailors. *(N. Bowdidge Collection)*

These views show two of the GER's shipping fleet known as saloon, light-draught paddle steamers, designed for operation on rivers such as the Orwell. Combined rail and boat excursions were very popular in the decade prior to the First World War. Harwich was one calling point on the route from Ipswich to Felixstowe for the SS *Norfolk* (184 ft long and 24 ft wide, gross tonnage 295 and 850 hp.) and for the smaller SS *Suffolk* (165 ft long, 21 ft wide, 245 tons and developing 650 hp). There were two classes of travel, fore cabin or saloon. The SS *Suffolk* was built in 1895 and the *SS Norfolk* in 1900. They were sold in 1931. There was a third vessel, the SS *Essex*, which was surplus to requirements and sold in 1913. *(N. Bowdidge Collection)*

NORFOLK

This view of Harwich signal-box must be later than 1953 because the brickwork around the base has been renewed following salt damage by floodwater in that year. The box closed 1 December 1985, the area being controlled by Parkestone. It is a good example of the 'cockscomb' roof style, and the box contained a fifty-lever McKenzie and Holland lever frame. *(N. Mundy/RCTS)*

Harwich Harbour, *c.* 1952. A mixed batch of wagons is being pushed over the adjustable bridge connecting the train ferry to the land. The wagons beyond the furthest ICI tanker are part of the raft which coupled to the pushing engine prevented too much weight being put on the bridge. The white vans belong to Le Société Belge-Anglaise des Ferry-Boats. *(HMRS)*

The forecourt at Hythe station is seen here in about 1900 before motorized transport had become the norm. *(Lens of Sutton)*

A gathering of railway staff on the platform at Brightlingsea station to mark the retirement of the stationmaster on 31 October 1924. *(Essex County Record Office)*

The opening ceremony of the Jaywick Sands miniature railway on 31 July 1936. This holiday attraction was an 18-in gauge line, which closed down when the Second World War started and never re-opened. The locomotive in view was based upon a GNR Stirling 'single driver' design and came, second-hand, from the Fairbourne miniature railway near Barmouth. It was built by Bagnall's in 1898. The line also possessed an oil-fired Sentinel type. *(Essex County Record Office)*

The pier at Walton-on-the-Naze included a ½-mile long electric tramway opened in 1898. There were three 'toastrack' carriages: one was for traction and there were two trailing cars. The tramway was replaced by a battery driven car in 1935. *(N. Bowdidge Collection)*

BIBLIOGRAPHY

Books

Branch Line Index, compiled by G.C. Lewthwaite (Branch Line Society, 1991)

British Independent Light Railways, John Scott-Morgan (David and Charles, 1980)

British Railways Atlas and Gazetteer (Ian Allan Publishing, 1973)

London, Tilbury and Southend Album, George Dow (Ian Allan Publishing)

Oxford Companion to British Railway History, Simmons and Biddle (Oxford University Press, 1997)

Locomotives of the LNER (RCTS, 1970)

A Regional History of the Railways of Great Britain, vol. 3, H.P. White, and vol. 5 D.I. Gordon (David and Charles, 1977)

Return to North Woolwich, compiled by GERS (PEMT Enterprises Ltd, 1987)

Periodicals

Backtrack (Atlantic Transport Publishers)

British Railway Journal (Wild Swan Publications)

British Railway Journal, Special Great Eastern Edition (Wild Swan Publications)

British Railways Illustrated (Irwell Press)

Bylines (Irwell Press)

GERS Journal and Information Packs (Great Eastern Railway Society)

HMRS Journal (Historical Model Railway Society)

Locomotives Illustrated (Ian Allan Publishing)

Railway Magazine (Ian Allan Publishing)

Railway Observer (RCTS)

Railways South East (Railways S.E.)

Steam Days (Redgauntlet Publications)

Trains Illustrated (Ian Allan Publishing)